See
Page 114

VIVID EXPOSURES

Jonathan W. Thompson, Editor

Vivid Exposures

Library of Congress
Cataloging in Publication Data

ISBN 0-7951-5088-1

Printed in China

Published by
The International Library of Photography
3600 Crondall Lane
Suite 101
Owings Mills, MD 21117

FOREWORD

Writing about photography is a difficult task, as it entails the translation of one art form into another. While every photograph may not inspire a thousand words, it is easy to see how the saying evolved. Words are a function of the intellect. But, much like music, a visual image speaks directly to the emotions, evoking an immediate and powerful response. Only when one attempts to analyze, interpret, and critique this image do words come into play.

As one views a photograph, one is slowly taken on a visual journey through the eye of the photographer. Whether the photograph was staged or the "point-and-click method" was employed, the picture represents the fact that moments in time pass within the blink of an eye. The photographer not only captures a scene or a subject; he also creates a lasting, tangible image of a fleeting instant. The beauty of photography is that any individual can produce an image of these passing moments.

Photography represents both an active and a passive art form. The degree to which a photographer participates in his art form varies from photograph to photograph. The photographer can either tell a story within the photograph, or simply stand aside and record life as it happens. The one thing that holds true for all photography is this: without the photographer there can be no photograph. Even in a simple snapshot, the photographer's influence is clearly evident.

The photographs within this anthology exhibit their own importance as well as demonstrate the importance of the photographer. In some cases, the idea or photo found the photographer. For instance, while taking pictures on a nature hike, a photographer may catch the sunset as it breaks through a bunch of trees, and thus an idea may be born. In other instances, a photographer may orchestrate and choreograph the set-up of a photograph in order to fulfill a creative idea or notion. (This may be the case in still-life or abstract photography.)

Another similar element in most of these photographs is the photographer's love of and dedication to his subject. For example, nature photography is often captured by devoted nature watchers. Those people who take humorous photographs usually enjoy the lighter side of life and tend to look for the funniest aspect of any situation. The numerous photographs of children in this book were most likely taken by parents or grandparents who appreciate the joy and wonderment contained in a child's smile. Becoming emotionally involved with a subject, through deep love or interest, often enables a photographer to generate ideas that help him capture the true essence of his subject.

There are also photographers who gain inspiration not from relating to one specific subject or another, but rather from focusing on the photographic process itself. They often use special techniques to create images they have envisioned within their own minds, or they choose to concentrate on one particular aspect of photography (such as lighting) and through experimentation examine its effect on a particular subject. By casting aside conventional approaches, these photographers open different pathways to new ideas, allowing their own imaginations to roam freely.

No matter how or why a photograph is taken, the viewer must realize that each photograph represents an individual's artistic viewpoint. There are many excellent photographs contained in this anthology. At a quick glance they might appear to be just pictures, but be sure to focus on the ideas being conveyed, both emotionally and physically. Allow yourself to become lost in the photo: perhaps you may gain a new understanding of it, or you may simply be able to relate more deeply to the photographer's viewpoint.

Andy Warhol once predicted that in the future everyone will have his fifteen minutes in the spotlight. This philosophy could easily be applied to photography by simply stating that every subject has its moment, and as a photographer, one must strive to find and capture these instants. After all, these cherished moments, which may seem frozen in time when we see them through the camera's viewfinder, do not last fifteen minutes; rather, viewing a photograph that captures these instances may trigger memories that will always remain embedded deep within our minds. Through photographs we are therefore offered a physical reminder as an accompaniment to a memory. We then hold in our hands the permanency of a cherished moment in time— an image of yesterday.

Russell Hall
Senior Editor

EDITOR'S NOTE

People have been constantly taught that they are complex beings, and that they should think complex thoughts and live their lives in complicated ways. By the same token, many photographers bury their subject in obscure imagery or clutter in order to convey their meaning in a way that may seem more intellectual or artistic. However, in the photographer's daily effort to produce the perfect image—an image that emits emotion and creates a dramatic effect that the viewer can understand and connect with no matter what the subject—it is often a simple image rather than an elaborate one that becomes the successful photograph. This is because a simple image often has one area of focus, offering little distraction, and when coupled with a strong subject, can be more striking than an image that took hours to create. As it is not in our nature as humans to seek out the smooth and natural, this task may seem very difficult. However, these images can be found anywhere—in a lake, a forest, a city, or even in your own home.

Simplistic images are effective because they work on a basic level that everyone can comprehend, often containing very fundamental elements such as color, light, and perspective. Usually these elements guide the viewer to a specific point in the photograph. The most effective of these points are often specific facial expressions and features, especially the eyes if the subject of the photograph is a person or animal, as they express an amazing amount of emotion and detail. Using these elements and allowing few or no distractions leaves little room for misinterpretation, while still allowing space for the viewer to develop their own ideas about the photograph.

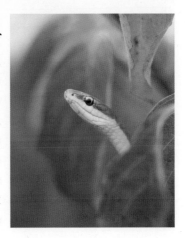

Garry Walter's Grand Prize Winning photograph, "Green Snake In Fall Leaves," is a wonderful example of how a simple image can also be a striking one. As we look at this photograph, two things stand out. The first is the striking yet fundamental use of contrasting colors—the vibrant red leaves surrounding the crisp green, yellow, and white of the snake's scales. Oftentimes colors can cause distractions within a photograph, but these colors are so sharp and crisp, and the red is so enveloping that you have no choice but to focus on the snake. The second thing that stands out is the snake's eye, which, upon looking at the photo, one's eye is immediately drawn to. The eye is so piercing, so solidly focussed, and the head so strong, that we easily gain a respect for this creature and its territory. But the most important thing we should notice about the image is its simplicity. In this photo, we are able to witness a quiet moment in the life of a snake, and with no distractions, are able to easily picture this snake on its daily cruise through the leaves, hiding from predators or in search of food.

While a color photograph has more opportunity to distract the viewer as stated earlier, black-and-white is less distracting because it works on the gray scale. In her untitled photograph, First Prize Winner Kelyn Akuna uses black-and-white photography to portray this image of a caged leopard, and, as you can see, the sharp contrast of the black on light gray plays an important role in attracting the viewer's attention to particular areas on the photograph. Also the crisp image fills the entire frame of the photograph so as not to allow for distractions, again drawing the viewer to specific points on the photograph. Like Garry Walter's photograph, the eye draws your immediate attention, almost pulling you inside the fence. The staring eye is so cold and powerful, and seems to be so intently fixed on the viewer that

we can feel the strength the animal has and can imagine its desire to be freed from behind the fenced boundaries. This simple yet dramatic depiction screams of the unfounded need people have to remove wild creatures from their natural habitat and put them on display. But even through this fence we can feel that this caged animal retains the fierce, powerful nature on which it survived in the wild.

Martin Maniewski on the other hand utilizes a simple cool green to color his First Prize Winning photograph, "Jilted," which creates a very calm, soothing affect. The girl fills the majority of the viewfinder so the viewer won't be distracted by outside objects. This image is very uncomplicated; no fancy techniques were used, but the angle from which the photo was taken, along with the cool green, creates a stunning affect. Again you may notice that her green glowing eyes are an important focal point. Though her body posture seems listless, her eyes stare through the viewer emotionlessly. Had this photograph been done in regular color or black-and-white, it more than likely would not have been as effective. The coloration provides us with deep green shadows and glowing yellow surfaces, leaving tinted green eyes and lips and a face half in shadow and half in light, enhancing the visual affect that she is looking directly at the viewer. The cool relaxing colors and the green of her eyes almost create a mesmerizing affect as she stares calmly up at the viewer.

An image of simplicity doesn't always need to be sought out, but can be as easy to find as childhood innocence in your own home. Courtney Ruge's Second Prize Winning photograph, "A Brother's Love," captured one of the simple moments shared between siblings. As we all know, sibling relations may not always be this friendly, but this one obviously depicts a moment of happiness that only children can enjoy. It is easy to tell that this is a moment of pure joy and love just by seeing the emotions emitted in the photograph and the expression on the little girl's face, in her eyes and smile. The use of black-and-white gives this loving image a more classic appeal, allowing us to think back to our own childhood and remember a moment similar to this: pushing your sister on the swing set, splashing in a mud puddle with your brother, or going out for ice cream with a parent. In this simple moment, we have to look into the face of this little girl and wonder what playful scheme her brother is so secretly whispering in her ear.

As you can see, an image does not have to be complicated in order to be effective. The simple images in life are often the ones that stand out and have the most striking appeal, often resonating strong emotions no matter what the subject. However, these unaffected images often seem the most difficult to find in our cluttered, busy world. But these simple images are all around us: in the subway, on the city streets, by the lake out back, even in your own home. Take some time to observe the world around you, dig through its complexities, and find the images that mean the most, the simple moments in life.

I would like to thank the entire staff at The International Library of Photography for all of their time and effort. This book would not have been possible without the hard work of the judges, editors, administrative services staff, customer service representatives, data entry personnel, office administrators, and computer service and mail room staff. I would like to congratulate the winners as well as all of the photographers who contributed their work, and I wish you good luck in all your future endeavors.

Laura R. Cohen
Editor

Grand Prize Winner

Garry Walter   Nature
Green Snake In Fall Leaves

Hillary Owen   Humor
Do Not Use As Stairs

Bernie Boettcher   Action
Rush!

Sandra Wilhite   Children
If Only . . .

Antonio Garcia   People
Rock And Nail

Adam Boyle   Other
Prison Hallway

Michele Hollenbach   Animals/Pets
Pride Of The Jungle

Dean Chetkovich   Sports
Let's Get This Race Started

Elizabeth McLearie   Animals/Pets
Highland Cow

Genevieve Leiper   Nature
Bridge To Nowhere

Elizabeth Losch   Other
Untitled

Misha Grigoriev   Children
The Apprentice

Tammy Mendonca   Children
That Special Moment

Rachel Glover People
Business Partners

James Noble Sports
Bubba With Bubba

Michelle Hawkins Nature
Aurora Canyon, Starved Rock State Park

Ryan T. Conaty People
Protesters At Republican National Convention, Philadelphia

Monica A. Hollenbeck Travel
Medieval Mirage

Dan Fameli People
Wishing For Spring

Jim Boemmels   Action
Ridin' High

Philip Munkacsy   Nature
Frog In The Pulpit

Masoud Amirloei   People
Hello And How Are You, Citizen?

S. Lim   Nature
Lizflower

Martin Maniewski   Portraiture
Jilted

Brandi Eilers   Animals/Pets
Jealousy

Sharon A. Stephens   Animals/Pets
Oh, Daddy . . .

Jennifer Reilly   Nature
Morning Dew

Jenn Szeker   Nature
Approaching Storm

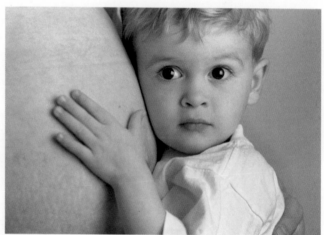

Dawn Stephani   Portraiture
Sister Paige

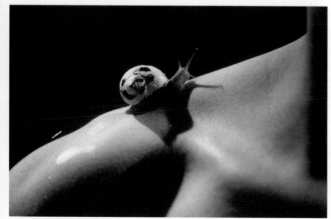

Spring Kunz   Other
Snail On Male

Catherine A. DiGiaimo   Children
Tea Party

Peter E. Jones   Travel
Nauset Light

Emily Skovira   Animals/Pets
Stolen Refreshment

Lanie Alexopoulos   Portraiture
Grandma's Moment

Amy Roberts   Sports
I'm Going To Hit This One!

Michael Pietrosante   Other
Guggenheim Afternoon

Loreen Berlin   Action
Up, Up, And Away

Debra Edgar Animals/Pets
Remember Me?

Kent Gunnufson Animals/Pets
Untitled

Katie Quayle Sports
Peter

Piotr Dras Other
The Rain Near The Colosseum

Mindy Pollock People
Finding Myself

Aylin Marcelo People
Diego And Julia

Adrienne Dicecco   Other
Door Of Rodin Museum

Tim Grey   Nature
Twisted

Brenda Whaley   Other
Ring

Simon Hawkins   Children
Tennis Friends

Ken Loeber   Nature
Hyakutake And The Crosses

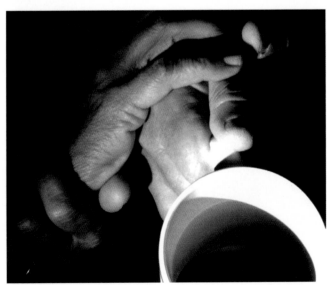

Joao Vaz   Other
One Coffee For Two

Lindsay Gibson   Children
Untitled

Lisa Etherton   Children
Mischievous Smile

Jimmy Smith   Travel
Looking Through A Window

Kelly Bruggema   Portraiture
Untitled

Courtney Ruge   Children
A Brother's Love

Dottie Doucette   Animals/Pets
Just The Two Of Us

Elizabeth Duncan People
Uighur Boy In Kashgar, China

Shari Abercrombie People
Good Luck, Girls! The Tossing Of The Bouquet

Melanie Harding Animals/Pets
Creature Comfort

Anne Meyer Portraiture
Michelle With Feathers

Julie Wheeler Children
This Little Piggy Cried All The Way Home

Kristen Bowlby Animals/Pets
Slurpin'

Vincent Lipford   Children
Mama's Little Girl

Eva Depoorter   People
At The Edge Of Time, A Light

Elizabeth Fleming   People
The Dress

Nancy Hadaway   Animals/Pets
Vantage Point

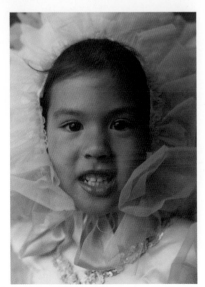

David Klaehn   Children
Marina

Jayson Hadwick   Portraiture
Heather

Britta-Lena Lasko   Other
Trumpeting Eggplants

James A. Bullard   Animals/Pets
G'Day, Mate

Mary E. M. H.   People
Dancing Girl

Garry Walter   Nature
Green Snake In Fall Leaves

Lynne Heroux   Travel
The Wall, Washington D.C.

Nikole Rae Rose   Travel
Puerta Azul—Old Mesilla, New Mexico

Tori Thompson Children
Don't You Wish You Still Had This Much Fun?

Logan Boon Nature
Passionately Pink

Bob Scholl Animals/Pets
Contentment

Ken Weissleder Sports
Gee, I Am Glad I Chose This Outfit

Shelly Corson Animals/Pets
Looking Through The Bars

Lou Deugarte Travel
Reflections Of Ketchikan

Kelyn Akuna   Animals/Pets
Untitled

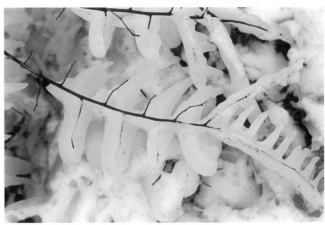

Thomas Polek   Nature
Untitled

Mercedes Fages   Travel
Solitude

Morgan Martinet   Children
Untitled

Elizabeth Wilson   Animals/Pets
Kitten On The Keys

Katherine Franz   Action
Pure Adrenaline

Mark Street   Nature
Reflections Of A Lady

Candice Winer   Animals/Pets
A Rainy Afternoon

Flavia Magno   Children
Little Girl

Gary Edmondson   Other
Searching

B. J. Thomas   Sports
A Moment Of Concentration

Bryan Martin   Animals/Pets
Oregon's King

Kevin Holznagle　　　　　　　　　　　　Animals/Pets
Life Is Great

Jorunn Irene Hanstvedt　　　　　　　　Animals/Pets
Dog Looking At Me

Heather Davenport　　　　　　　　　　Portraiture
In A Teenager's Eyes

Christina DuMong　　　　　　　　　　　Nature
The Perfect Strawberry Freed From An Imperfect World

Raymond Bowyer　　　　　　　　　　　Nature
Untitled

Ben Sterling　　　　　　　　　　　　　Sports
TD Mystery

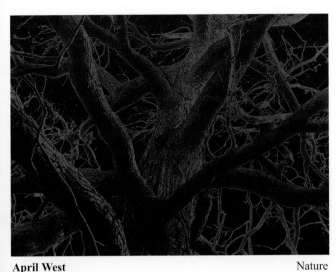

April West   Nature
Nature's Nerve

Maria Fernanda Hubeaut   People
La Tabaqueria, "The Cigar Factory"

Ash Daniel   People
Father And Son

Attila Fovenyessy   Portraiture
Performer Of The Great Singsing Of Goroka, 1994

Adam Glickman   Other
Untitled

Matthew D. Johnson   Other
Boot In A Cave

Nicholas Lennon   Children
Monkey Business

Natalie Vollmer-Sciscio   Humor
Portrait Of Frosty

Sarah Ellis   Children
Untitled

Florine Duffield   Humor
Here's Looking Up Your Address

L. A. Basilé   Nature
Iowa

Marlene Rounds   Portraiture
Angel—Self-Portrait

Cheuk-Bor Chu   Portraiture
Man Performing

Maurine Reier   Humor
Hangin' On In Texas

Molly Kearney   Portraiture
Visions Of A Mockingbird

John Banach   Sports
Ferrari Returns To Indianapolis

Cyril Fernandez   People
Students On Strike

Bea Ahbeck   Humor
Nuns Playing Ball

Geraldine M. Ross   Animals/Pets
Daydreams

Cynthia Allen   Nature
Majestic

Stephanie Silver   Nature
Indiana Summer

Marilyn Underwood   People
Playing In The Leaves

Yael Wolf   Animals/Pets
Take Me With You!

Lora Pastore   Animals/Pets
Hey, Who Stole My Fish?

Robert R. Dyck   Nature
Light, Shadow, Reflection

Catharine Anastasia   Nature
Sunset Church

Vicki Stevens   Animals/Pets
Babe Waiting For Her Treat

Vonita Pitt   Humor
True Love

Sandra Couch   Animals/Pets
Oh, What A Relief!

Anne W. McClure   Nature
Nature's Window

Arlene M. Holcomb People
Hi, Baby Bird

Jacob Edmondson Nature
The Start Of A Beautiful Day

Shirley L. Other
Sunset In The City

Leah McCoy Nature
Untitled

Harold E. Bohm Nature
Bridge Over The Big Thompson

Jeanette Nejame Children
My Sister And Me

Katie Chambers   Children
Dandelion Delight

Carlos Aciar   Children
Infancy

Bertha Scotten   Children
Grandma's Twin Delights

Jeanene Weidman   Children
Boy, It's Great To Be A Kid!

Anita Bergman   Other
Lady By The Lake

Sherri Warren   Children
Back 4 More

Ronald Woodcock   Animals/Pets
Cozy Kitties

Patricia Anderson   Nature
A Cloud In The Sky

Anya Warda   Other
Who Are You?

Aaron Truax   People
The Love Pinch

Frank Hawrylo   Children
Stephie And Jacob

Robert Napolitano   Animals/Pets
Wish To Fly Like A Bird

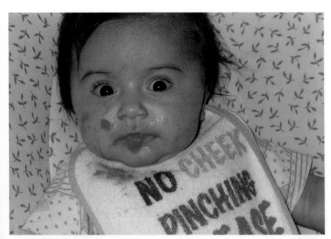

Mary P. Mitchell   Children
What, We're Having Squash!

John D. Mitchem   Nature
Olmstead Falls

William B. Lewis   Other
Looking Toward The Future!

Jen Messinger   People
Dreamers

Larry Anderson   Travel
Reflections

Jennifer L. M. Godfrey   Animals/Pets
Bedtime?

Shawna Marie Landis Other
Fisgard Lighthouse

Rosalee Harney Animals/Pets
Irish Eyes Are Smiling

Jim V. Coffey Nature
True Faith

Jenny Henry People
A Tribute To Elvis

Veronica H. Czachur Nature
Untitled

Deanna Garvin Gould Animals/Pets
Duncan's Love

Jean Lentini   Animals/Pets
Little Pebbles

Jurgen Brian   Animals/Pets
Raven, WWII War Dog Reenactor

Lisa Maurer   Children
First Blush

Cathy Roskaz   People
Love

Michelle Veliz   Children
Anyone Can Do Anything

Laurie Harris   Animals/Pets
Scout

Michelle McFarland People
Unconditional Love

Sue Bruning People
Bonding

Gary B. Messinger Children
Eyes Of Wonder

Joy Johnsen Children
Fearless Beauty—Samantha Joy Fox

Zakia Williams Travel
Downtown Atlanta Skyline

Robin Zeller People
Sharing A Father And Son Moment

Lora J. Powers People
Right Place At The Right Time

Mary Rayburn Children
Anticipation Of Adventure

Elaine Simcoe People
Walk In The Woods

Helen Gruenhagen Animals/Pets
Buddies To The End

Hope Robson Wolsegger Children
Falling Down In Leaves

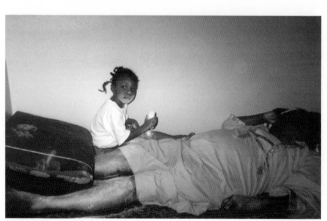

Martistine Wade-Goode Children
Caught In The Act

Laura Thompson   Travel
Peaceful Juggernauts

Wayne R. Hardy   Travel
Summer Palace—Beijing

Ida S. Hudson   Children
Joyous Moments

Deborah Coates   Nature
Wagner Falls

Rebecca Fischer-Miller   Children
First Steps

Betsy Pentecost   Humor
What Sign?

Martha Long   Nature
A Moment That Lasted Forever

Elaine Gordon   Children
On The Line

Matthew LaPat-Fier   Animals/Pets
My Dog, Ruffy

Laura E. Spaulding   Animals/Pets
Lonely Dreamer

Gi-Gi Plowden   Animals/Pets
Bed Partners

Kim Keiser   Nature
What's Up?

Victoria Belzer-Wood   Nature
Calling Thee Home

David J. Jordan   Nature
After The Rain

Sondra Stephens   Children
Children Of Honduras

Edmund Ryder   Animals/Pets
Gooney Birds On Guard At Midway Island, SW Pacific

Julia A. Pollard   Children
Hmm! What's On Sale?

Melody M. Polak   Children
Our Lovable Bunny

Harriet Coleman   Animals/Pets
Squirrel Watching

Wynne Wigderson   Travel
Michigan Sunset

Grazyna Kus   Animals/Pets
Nicky's Little Angel

Debra E. Sanford   Nature
One Winter's Day

Rachel Smith   Children
Twisting For Daddy

Claudia Howe-Harbut   Nature
McLean Game Refuge

Lou-Ann Merrell   Other
Raising Old Glory—A Son's Eagle Scout Project

Rosemary Pozzi   People
Friends Forever

Evelyn Elschlager   Animals/Pets
Could That Be A Bee?

Idell Dearry   Children
Shaping Up

Valerie D. Beasley   People
Queen Of The Nile

Gladys Disidore   Animals/Pets
Say Cheese

Eva V. Meakin   Animals/Pets
Precious Moments

Erinn Stryzewski   Nature
Morning Mist

Eugene J. Koster   Travel
Twin Towers, New York

Barbara Dutcher   Animals/Pets
Blind Dog With Baby Deer

Diane Howard   Animals/Pets
Great-Horned Sheep

Perry Blatstein   Sports
Basketball At Its Best

Jackie Dulgerian   People
Relaxing By The Ocean

Becky McLaughlin   Travel
Mystery Mountain

Joshua D. Knecht   Nature
A Sweet Kiss Good Night

Barbra Roser   Children
Summer's End

Lucille Daigle   Other
Field Of Dreams

Adrienne Avery   Children
Lovable Avery

Eve Faith Children
A 1950 Hootenanny

Dana Cart Action
Arrow In Flight

Edna Hill Nature
Car Tracks

Cheryl Bugieda Nature
A Lovely Day For Ducks

Victory Phillips Children
Looks Normal To Me

Gracie Shrader Nature
Panama City, FL, At Magnolia Campground

Bridget Roun   Animals/Pets
Home From The River

Marge Hemsworth   Nature
Sunset At Lion's Bay

Gisele Kern   Nature
Bird's-Eye View

Angela J. Scheetz   People
Hand In Hand

Kenneth Bostick   Nature
Early Morning

Darla Jackson   Children
Double Trouble

Erica Mooney　　　　　　　　　　　Children
Face-To-Face With Fall

Amy Winterrol　　　　　　　　　　Animals/Pets
Reilly On Memorial Day

Delema T. Reed　　　　　　　　　　Travel
Going Home

Diane Cooper　　　　　　　　　　Children
My Little Pumpkin

Peggy Smotherman　　　　　　　　Nature
First Snow

M. Soultanis　　　　　　　　　　People
Loving Faith

Maureen A. Suit   Other
Winter Morn

Joan M. Brunelle   Travel
Mount St. Michael's Abby Church

Thomas Stevens   Children
Sleepy Bugs

Suszette Henry   Animals/Pets
The New Generation

Joseph E. Moore   Children
My, Am I Surprised!

Tina M. Garcia   Children
Country Morning

Gayle E. Kassak   Nature
Fall Fashions For 2000

Charlie Giacomarra   Travel
Marblehead Lighthouse

Francis J. Toomey   Animals/Pets
My Wild Rabbit Likes Crackers

Lacie Sumrall   Animals/Pets
Boot Camp

Ronald Landry   Children
Summer Innocence

Helen Cheng   Nature
The Grand Canyon Of Yellowstone

Lanette Barnes Humor
Pickle Tickles

John A. Harlacker Animals/Pets
Advertising Is For Everybody, Including My Pet Dog, Shep

Brandy Blount Travel
Paradise

Donna Spencer Nature
Arizona's Beauty

Christel Axtell Children
Chilling With My Baby Calf

Mary Harris Nature
Barbed Winter

Henry J. Fleiner Other
Caroline's Summertime Hideaway

Julie Hohn Nature
Firestorm

Jodi Kukla Travel
Passion, Excitement, And Anticipation For The First Cast

Christine Janes Children
Oops!

Laura L. Foulke Animals/Pets
A Close Encounter

Jennifer Howland Children
Pea Pod Lindsay

Patty J. Evans   Animals/Pets
Thor Smelling A Flower

Barbara Lanzendorfer   Nature
In The Eyes Of The Beholder

Deanna Butka   Children
The Boat Ride

Cheryl LeBlanc   Nature
Oh, Deer

Betty D. Austin   Other
Springhouse

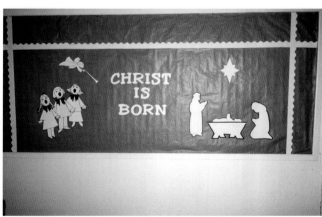

Andrew L. Farrar   Other
Christ Is Born

Yvonne J. Boyd   Nature
Roadside Forager

Theresa Booker   Children
Best Friends Wishing

Elizabeth Boyle   Animals/Pets
Jailhouse Rock

Julie Ann Luke   Nature
No Trespassing

Romona J. Westerfield   Animals/Pets
An American Cat

Deborah Ann Taigaafi   Children
Puyallup Fair

Dawn Coughlin   Children
Twin Sisters At The Cape

Vesta Buffo   Animals/Pets
Ariel, The Toy Poodle, And Her Favorite Mouthful

Elizabeth Newberg   Travel
Ana

Tricia DeVries   Travel
Vegas Lights

Angelia Hall   Animals/Pets
Best Friends

Julie Hunt   Animals/Pets
Fancy In The Grass

Tom Gildea   Nature
Falls Of Eden

Julia S. Espeland   Other
Gibraltar Lighthouse

Marilyn K. Ratliff   Nature
Tranquil Stream

Kris Pease   Animals/Pets
Gentle Cycle, Please

Tammy Ray   Animals/Pets
Ponies Of Assateague

Kristi Berland   Animals/Pets
The Fisherman

Randy Crouch   Animals/Pets
Best Buddies

Riva E. Esrig   Nature
Majestic Splendor

Mark Ritter   Other
Old Time Firefighting

Lauri Richardson   Nature
God's Gift

Colleen J. Keller   Nature
Peace In The Valley

Eric Robinson   Nature
The Watchman At Zion Canyon National Park

Charles Johnson   Nature
Topiary Of Clouds

Rhonda McCarter   Travel
The Splendor Of Switzerland

Claire Rose   Travel
Tied Up

Betty L. Eaton   Children
We're Glad We Are Americans!

James Butterfield   Animals/Pets
Woe Is Me

Olivia M. Chicoine   Children
Beloved Nephew

Jennifer L. Lewis   People
Washed Out

June Rowley   Animals/Pets
Cinder Jumps For Joy

Sandra McLean   Children
Tracker

Verna Myers   Children
Unclaimed Melody

Joseph McGrath   Humor
I'm On Top Of The World

Carle Dwyer   Children
Determination

Frosty Buck   Animals/Pets
First Day At School

Dorothy Oliver   People
Mother, Daughter, And Grandson

Nicole Campbell   Animals/Pets
Mother Lexus And Pup

Libbie Robinson   Other
Okay, Daddy, I Got It! Let Me Try!

Sandra Skrocki   Children
Nantucket Memories

Kimberly Dubois   Nature
Can You See Me?

Cherry L. Toland   Animals/Pets
Forty!

Daria Sinnott   Travel
Dawn In Alaska

Ricky Lee Browning   Animals/Pets
Little Bear

John L. Galle Sr.   People
Not To Worry, It's Only A Fire Drill

Michael Warren   Other
Struggling With Decisions

Margaret Sneed   Nature
Sunset On Lake Pontchartrain

Laurel Taylor   Animals/Pets
Baby Moose In Mountain Marsh

Haroula Dias   Animals/Pets
Jake Looking Into The Distance

Lestie Holmes   Other
June Sunrise In Denver

Amanda Safford   Animals/Pets
Not Easily Bribed

Julia Gines   Nature
Vision Of Peace II

Rosemarie Sauerzopf   Travel
Beach At Lake Maggiore

Nancy J. Rapalee   Nature
Home For The Night

Shelley L. Williams   Animals/Pets
Let's Be Friends!

C. C. Cheng   Animals/Pets
Morning Visitors

F. L. Schick   Nature
Beauty Of Pisgah National Forest

Yvonne Marie Oliver   Travel
Bahama Sunset

Heather Gunn   Nature
Liftoff

Earl Appin   Nature
Morning Dew

Lester Kimmel   Animals/Pets
Corncob Lunch

Joanne Cunningham   Animals/Pets
Dozer With His Lollipop

Dorothy G. Martin   Nature
Promises

Kate Lynn Stonehocker   Nature
The Calm Before The Storm

Winifred Cunnigham   Children
Concentration

Jennifer Babcock Nature
Beauty Of The Bayou

Susan M. Oliver Nature
The Magic Of Springtime

Wayne Sennholz People
I'm Guarding The Queen

B. J. Perez Travel
A Cuban Church

Jamie Struthers Animals/Pets
Wildebeest Migration

Jan Kusner Nature
Ending Of An Autumn Day

Roma Hoff   People
Clara—Newborn And At Four Years Old

Dee Reynolds   Children
Child Building Sand Castle

Michele Ballinger   Nature
Hiding In Plain Sight

J. Lynn Ringeling   Animals/Pets
Enouk—Beluga Whale

William Bevan   Sports
Fly-Fishing Boy

Shelby Pannell   Animals/Pets
Hiding From Mother

Joann Michl　　　　　　　　　　　　　Nature
Beauty At Rest

Robin S. Murray　　　　　　　　　　　Nature
Dolphin Trio

Suzanne Troy　　　　　　　　　　　　Nature
My Sanctuary

Sharon E. Brown　　　　　　　　Animals/Pets
Little Pooh And Friend

Blondale Sandritter　　　　　　　　Portraiture
Sitting Pretty

Mary L. Scott　　　　　　　　　　　　Action
Too Beautiful To Stand Still

John Balyo   Children
Butterfly

Priscilla Fletcher   Animals/Pets
Sweet Dreams

Nancy Schoedel   Humor
Dad Helping His Daughter Bowl For The First Time

Lu-Anne Papeo   Nature
Untitled

Tyler Knight   Animals/Pets
Mr. Blue Jay

Leo Bagley   Nature
Double Blessing

Jimmy Collins   Children
"Oh, Say Can You See . . ."

Kathleen Mack Riha   Nature
The Falls—Watkins Glen, NY

Josephine Heitzman   Animals/Pets
Harmony

Paula Gillenwater   Animals/Pets
A Pot Of Cat

Amanda Lin Smith   Other
Inspiration Point

Margaret Mitchell   Nature
Sunset 2000

Dennis Thurston   Animals/Pets
Togetherness

Gerald J. Vilendrer   Animals/Pets
A Shepherd And His Flock

Nell Tedford   Nature
Nature's Splendor

Ramona Pehowski   Nature
Keyhole View Of Autumn

Anne D. Holland   Travel
Autumn In Mystic

Matthew Yough   Travel
Home

Rhoda Woodward　　　　　　　　Animals/Pets
A Lucky Shot

Michael W. Joslyn　　　　　　　　Sports
One More Inch

Geraldine Modrell　　　　　　　　Nature
Peacefulness

Marie Saunders　　　　　　　　Nature
God Put A Rainbow In The Sky

Robert L. Mellema　　　　　　　　Children
Sabrina Kay

Sharon Kerkman　　　　　　　　Animals/Pets
Here's Looking At You, Kid

Alfredo Mancuso   Other
Spirit Of Man

Chongren Yu   Children
I Will Win

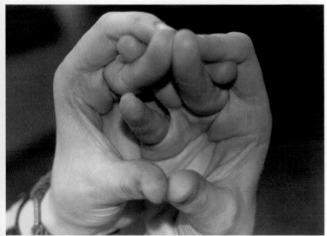

Christy Bowers   Other
The Snake

Koli Leach   Animals/Pets
Please, Don't Throw My Pillow

Zela Cole   Nature
Fall In The West Virginia Hills, Summersville Lake

Jeanne Rippey   Nature
The Sun Caught Floating In The Clouds Above Sedona

Donna Wilson   Animals/Pets
Standing Guard

Stefani Lukaszewski   Nature
Unbelievable

Cherie Burrows   Sports
Winter Sports

Lisa Bailey   Children
At First Sight

Lois G. Ripley   Other
Thready With Pane

Linda Cabaniss   Animals/Pets
You've Got Mail!

Iwona Korus   Travel
Hollywood

Cherri Kraus   People
My Marlboro Man

Shannon Pappalardo   People
A Grandson's Love

George T. Carr   Nature
Good Morning For The Jersey Shore

Sandra Neely   Nature
Serenity At Sunrise

Darrell Hennion   Portraiture
Star Of My Life

Betty J. Altland   Animals/Pets
What Do I See?

Keith Medinas   Nature
Autumn's Gift

Irene Foster   Nature
Arctic Moon

Sonia M. Spires   Children
Ben

Allan R. Way   People
Where Is This Train Going?

Alfredina Kannes   People
Matilda's Tomatoes

Irene Schulz   Other
Cat In Canopy Bed

Christine M. Vogt   Animals/Pets
Rainbow Lovebirds

Arnold R. Gustke   Animals/Pets
Boots

Amie Leeds   Other
Philadelphia Freedom

Melissa Stephan   Other
Times Gone By

Billie A. Foulger   Nature
Teton Magic

Marlyss Ermert   Nature
Dominique In The Leaves

Lisa Harrison   Children
Snow Day

Julie Rose   Nature
End Of A Beautiful Day

Shawn Buss   Nature
Mother Earth's Majesty

Andrew Meyer   Nature
Key West

Deborah J. McNichols   Nature
Pristine Perfection

William McLeod   Travel
Once Upon A Time

Julie Best   Nature
Wonders Of Alaska

Helen L. Weitz   Portraiture
Angels Among Us

Julie Beetle   Travel
Peaceful Journey

Marion Rupert   Animals/Pets
Alaska

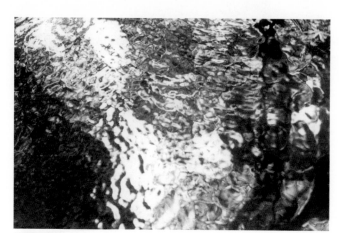

Tiffany Horn   Nature
Liquid Silver

Emily A. Weiss Humor
So There!

Theo Parquet Children
Our Little Mouse

Vera L. Perry Nature
Face Of The North Wind

Rachael Feliciano Animals/Pets
". . . And One For All!"

Florence LaEzza Nature
Early Morning Dew

Lori Abbott Travel
View From Cabbage Island, Maine

Anita Ogline   Nature
Sunset Over The Grand Tetons

Carol Hosting   Nature
Reflections

Denis A. Simmons   Nature
Sunset At Sand Point

Pam Hillage   Nature
Morning Tranquility

Kimberly Todd   Nature
Be Still And Know I Am God

Elissa Holtmeier   Nature
Nature's Christmas Gift

T. George Tyborski   People
Summer Serenity 2000

Lorri Blazer   People
Fishing Buddies

Elaine T. Bilodeau   Nature
The Kennebec River

Karen Watson   Nature
Unexpected Rainbows

Eric Spaeth   Action
Boundary Waters

Norma L. Ford   Travel
Bluebird's Trip To West Virginia

Alex Yount Travel
The Lady On Liberty Island

Jeannette M. Large Nature
Bird In Flight

Dee Schander Children
Cory In A Wave

Crystal Speicher Nature
The Unforgettable Moment

Lacita A. McDonald Nature
Nature's Deceiving Wonders

Joan Culwell Nature
Colorado High Country

Kyle B. Thomas Travel
Empyrean Image

Jennie Romanelli Animals/Pets
Spike

Kathleen Harris Nature
Late Autumn Sunset

Virginia Fantarella Nature
Sundown At Chapoquoit

Rosette Jones Other
For The Love Of The Sun

Linda L. Bertiaux Animals/Pets
Silhouetted Pennsylvania Elk

Karen J. Boyd   Action
Shadows In The Night

Craig Bush   Other
Meph

Becky Kilian   Nature
Our Lord's Promise

Kathleen J. Carlson   Nature
Bremerton Ghost Ship

Catherine Vanderbosch   Nature
Wyoming Windmill

Richard F. Windsor   Other
Fourth Of July At Chautauqua

Dianna Neal   Nature
Fury In Green

Amanda Batts   Animals/Pets
Catnap

Courtney Charest   Nature
Life's Second Chances

Darcy L. Brummund   Nature
Phoenix Sunset

Sharion Otey   Other
Cotton Candy In The Sky

Mary E. Smith   Children
Treasures

James Lee Smith People
Smith Brothers Four

Mary Ellen Leeper Travel
Nature's Accident

Mamie T. Thomas Nature
Sunset In Moreno Valley, CA

Sheila Rossi Nature
Reflections

Marjory Schultz Nature
Shining On The Tree Line Across The Lake

Harold Teller Animals/Pets
Josie

Elena Prehoda   Animals/Pets
Hello There

David Segal   Travel
Eiffel Tower Lights, 2000

April Brown   Children
Cruising

Michael D. McCarron   Nature
Red Skies At Night

J. Phillip Drinnon   Nature
Poisonous Loser

Harland Cashman   Nature
Morning Fog On Lake Bomoseen, Vermont

Karen Foster   Action
Spring Fever

Sherry Palenius   Animals/Pets
From The Heavens

Mel Sinclair   Children
Breath Of Spring

Vicki L. Derr   Animals/Pets
Cow-Gone, Take Me Away

Dilip Panakkal   Nature
Fire Mountain

Anne Welsh   Travel
Solitude In Scotland

Thomas Balfe   Travel
Night Falls

Hilda Sakowsky   Other
Night Shots

Shelly Eckel   Animals/Pets
Hide-And-Seek

Martha G. Howell   Other
Mountain Majesty

Anthony R. Scopellite   Travel
A Lasting Tribute

Tracy W. Williams   Other
Ray Of Hope

Frank Sollecito   Other
Arizona Landscape North Of Flagstaff

Elizabeth C. Gumbart   Nature
Green On Gray—Denali National Park

Paul Donais   Nature
Harbor Lights

Penny Pomeranz   Animals/Pets
Hide-And-Seek

Denise Boege   Travel
An Afternoon Diversion

Antonio D. Salcedo   Nature
Radiant Wave

Randy Costantino   Children
Microscopes

Pati Harris   Children
This Pumpkin

Robert J. Levin   Travel
Pemaquid

Kathy Papan   Animals/Pets
Chanook

Tom Claes   Nature
Omaha Beach, September 2, 1997

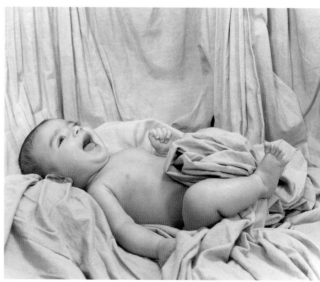

Henry Quintero   Portraiture
Henry Jr.—Premature Baby

Kevin O'Farrell   Children
Captured Moment

Mindy McBride   Other
Pots Of The Past

Andrew David Farina   Nature
Dusk

Deborah K. Jones   People
Omniscience

Virginia L. Morris   Children
A Carefree Moment

Lou LaPolla   Nature
Early Morning

Stephanie L. Watson   Nature
Niagara Falls

Nancy D. Hardin   Nature
Electrified Rainbow

Claudette Gross   Children
Pure Joy

Rose M. Riviezzo   Nature
Tulip In Snow

James H. Ware   Travel
Celtic Legacy

Sara E. Burkhart   Nature
Over The Edge

Nick Nagle   People
Gramma's Birthday

Carrie Phelan   Nature
Ray Of Hope

Jennie Persicano   Humor
First Date

Carol Luongo   Nature
Tranquility In Florida

Humberto Mendoza   Animals/Pets
Ocean Life

Eura Foster   Nature
Early Morning On The Farm

Christopher Arthur Cox   Nature
Raven's View—Grand Canyon

Nancy Fenical-Kohler   Nature
Winter '99

Judith Messier   Animals/Pets
It's A Good Life

Kathryn Sammons   Nature
Lovin' Lichens

Barbara Aitken   Travel
Monument Valley

Charla Blackmon   Nature
Sunset On The Nile

Carol Ann Pavlich   Nature
Nature's Mysteries

Yolanda Graham   Sports
Freedom

Doug Siegel   Nature
Face In The Mountain

Diane McCray   Nature
Fall Splendor

Marion T. Porrino   Animals/Pets
Baby's First Snow Run

Myron Woods   Nature
Sunset During A Storm In Iowa

Anthony Harris   Children
Blooming With Personality

Ronald Croteau   Travel
Kennicott—Historic Alaskan Mine

Karina Muenchow   People
Suspended In Time

Betty M. Welsh   Animals/Pets
First Modeling Job

David E. Mason   Nature
Jacob's Ladder

Jan Egger   Nature
The Viking

Stephanie Humphrey-Johnson   Children
Wat Phu Kids

Mitchel Libman   Animals/Pets
Rain Dance

Robert G. Gilman   Animals/Pets
Home, Sweet Home

Teresa Vance   Humor
Satisfaction

Tonya B. Teal   Children
Fall Characters

Frances Brigid Hargreaves   Nature
Sunset Over Lake Ray Hubbard

Helen Overton   Animals/Pets
Aphid Inspector

Attila Fovenyessy   Portraiture
Kila From The Huli Tribe—Papua New Guinea, 1994

Nichole Norell   Nature
In Dreams

Teresa Menard   Children
Gabriel

Mike Esterline   Nature
Reflections

Peggy J. Howard   People
Independence

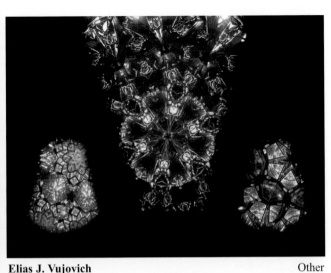

Elias J. Vujovich   Other
Modern Day Single Parent With Offspring

Jody Scott   Children
Little Miss Jr. Naturalist

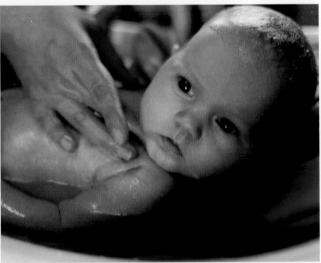

Yulanda J. Chapman   People
Dominique Rose Chapman

Michael W. Cater   Nature
Comet Hyukatake, Spring 1996

Marilyn B. Lee   Nature
Memories Of Asbury Park

Janice N. Cannella   People
Ghost Riders—Shadows Of Freedom

93

Rodger Jackson
Animals/Pets
Sunning By The Sea

Colleen L. Isdale
Animals/Pets
Nanny And Oreo

Melissa Spooner
Animals/Pets
Feeding Frenzy

June C. Sebesta
Travel
Christmas Holiday Mall

Rosemary Dunwell
Children
Autumn's Joy Child

Jennifer Ann Teske
Nature
Black-Eyed Susans

Barbara Richardson   Travel
Olcott Interlude—Duluth, MN

Linda Pyle   Other
Serenity

Joseph P. Barnes   Animals/Pets
The Chickens Come Home To Roost

Erin Travis   People
Friendship

Kay Goodman   Travel
Beach At Monterosso, Italy

Helen M. Fields   Children
Ready To Play

Lorraine Bloemer   Children
The Little Clown

Colleen Mitton   Nature
Hidden Beauty

Shelley S. Edwards   Children
Wetter Wonderland

Tina Anderson   Animals/Pets
Lone Spirit

Donald Halls   Action
Fire On The Overpass

Thomas Clyde Melton   Other
Sacrifice Touching Liberty

Carolyn Pelletier   Humor
The Gift—Sight Of The Angel Boy

Pepper Adair   Animals/Pets
For Mom On Christmas

Jean Bartkowiak   Nature
Up-North Happiness

Marguerite F. Farmer   Nature
Monterey, 2000

Judy Johnson   Nature
Serenity At Sunset

Donna Morrow   Nature
Polar Bear On The Ice Flow In Barrow, AK

Michael McGuire   Children
Untitled

Stacie Pelegrinis   Other
What A Catch!

Meredith Duval   Travel
Sailing Into The Sunset

James Nolan   Nature
A Fall Day In Southern New England

Tabitha Thayer   Travel
Holland Sailing Adventure

Waldemar Poppe   People
Our Little Mermaids

Justin Saksenberg   People
Best Friend

Frances Harris   Animals/Pets
I'm Sorry I Made A Mess Of Your Garbage

Lisa A. King   Animals/Pets
Hoo's Watching?

Nancy Purinton   Animals/Pets
Maisie, July Fourth

Alexis Kauriga   Nature
Emerald Waters

Kathleen Shaw   Nature
Good Morning Sunshine

Brenda Wills — Children
Peek-A-Boo

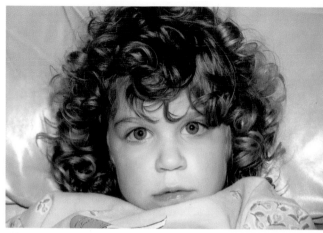

Alex Lenda — Children
In From The Cold

Claudia E. Gehm — Nature
A Sky Blue Sea

Ruth Knoll — Children
A Minute Of Silence

Danielle Trnka — Animals/Pets
Armrest

Al Johnson — Travel
Are You Looking At Me?

Irene Trombino   Travel
Caves Of The Dead Sea Scrolls, Israel

Gayla Lewis   Children
Second Base Angel

Donna Dougherty   Nature
God Is So Good

Emma Jane Silvaney   Children
Young Love—Precious Moments

Heather Granata   Animals/Pets
Lucky

Josephine Kowaleski   People
Great-Grandma's Pleasure

Ethel B. D. Lange   Nature
October Shoreline On Beaver Island

Sam R. Lee   Nature
Spire At Sunset

Kathy Daboul   Nature
Sunset Silhouette

Jason Greer   Action
Big Bang

Terese Kane   Children
Tall Tails

Todd Wagner   People
Peaceful Moments

John W. Miracle Other
Walkway

Robert Bozant Nature
Strike A Pose

Kris Bark Portraiture
Yesterday's Warrior

Janett Burns Humor
Sorry, I Missed You!

Myriam Beigh Nature
Gull In Flight

Elizabeth Whitman Children
Princess At The Beach

Darlene Krueger   Animals/Pets
Magnificent Beauty

Chrissy Astbury   Other
Potz

Lee Wimberly   Other
Chair In Light

Pearl Jones   Other
The Millennium Ends

Gene Hannigan   Nature
Guardians Of The Steppes

Roy Hemmings   Travel
The Queen's Men

Bruce L. Husselman Nature
August Moon

Frank Jeffrey Suarez Onatra Nature
The Sun In A Hand

Marcella J. Ruble Animals/Pets
Great View With No Spray

Barbara Pasnik Nature
Calm Before The Storm

Irene Duarte Animals/Pets
Ft. Worth Duck Pond

Kenneth Franco Nature
Ducks At Sunrise

Frank Fernandes Portraiture
Is There Anybody Out There?

Lowell P. Forbes Nature
Afternoon On Redcloud Peak

Robyn McCluskey Nature
Midday Snack

Rocky Ruggiero Nature
Nature At Its Best

Kevin L. Raines Nature
Spring Of Life

Helen Kiser Nature
The Gathering

Stephen Pidliskey   Children
Time For Our Pedicure

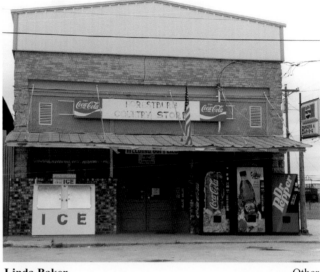

Linda Baker   Other
The Past And The Present

Carolyn Pete   Travel
Devil's Den, Gettysburg

Kristine Mershon   Nature
Grand Canyon—Eternal Awakening

Carol Sines   Nature
Golden Glory

Necias E. Usaraga   Nature
Beauty In God's Creation

Richard A. Lamb   Nature
Life Is Fragile In Sun Lakes, AZ

Parvin Darabi   Other
Mother And Child

Joseph Giordano   Nature
Impending Storm

Ann B. Durrigan   Nature
Pileated Woodpecker

Gary Hanna   Humor
Tell Me Again About Evolution

Sarah Lawson   People
Born In The South

Kay Knight People
Native American Tribal Dance

Laurie Jo Smith Children
First Snow

Lisa Clay Animals/Pets
Hacoona—Blizzard Of '96

Betty A. Holmes Animals/Pets
High Jump

Laura Spector Travel
Mystical Majesty

Joan Brooks Nature
Canadian Geese In Flight

Janice Hodkinson Nature
Kildeer Lodge

Barbara Roberts Nature
Reflections

Ashley Grasso People
Tranquil Moments

Judith Lubcher Nature
Sunflower Dreams

Carl E. Knudsen Animals/Pets
Clear, Cool Water

Mary M. Mehaffey Animals/Pets
Bottle, Please

Alberto E. Leopizzi   Nature
Diverse-A-Tree

Isabel Benitez   Children
Jackie's Ride

Ronnie Nasralla   Action
Dancers In Flight

Carla S. Frost   Nature
Phantom Of The Ice

Jennifer Nason   Nature
Casco Bay Sunset

Nichole Hurst   Nature
Sunset In The Smokies

Cynthia Fugere   Nature
Untitled

Lee Loring   Animals/Pets
The Lone Ranger

Pamela Sheetz   Animals/Pets
Am I Comfortable Or What?

Kathy Rapp   People
A Lesson In Life

Richard A. Moody   Animals/Pets
On The Wall

Allison Ratner   Nature
Pollination

Sandra Zaun — Travel
The Crossing

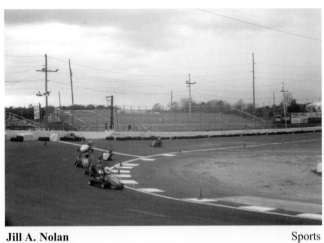

Jill A. Nolan — Sports
Go-Kart Racing In Riverhead, Long Island, New York

Rachel Campbell — Nature
Highlands Of Scotland

Lisa A. Miller — Travel
Oponohu Bay From Lookout Point Of Le Belvedere

Elizabeth Sensenig — Children
Brushing My Smile

Cathy Porter — Nature
Floriferous

Alison Walsh   Humor
No Wonder Greece Was The Cradle Of Civilization

Barbara Folks   Animals/Pets
Relaxing On A Long Hot Summer Day

Donald Elligan Jr.   People
Donese's First Pose

Linda Richardson   Animals/Pets
Together 'Til The End Of Time

Steve Kehoe   Nature
Once Upon A Wing

James E. Drasal   Travel
Los Cabos, Mexico

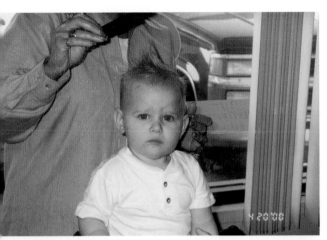

Ann Bailey Children
First Haircut

Fran Kennedy Animals/Pets
What . . . You Talking To Me?

Donald F. Loughry Nature
The Fall Of The Dandelions

Stoney Brooks Nature
Shoreline Contemplation

June Morgan Other
Memories

Marge Terrell Animals/Pets
Paradise At Last!

Melissa Tomhave   Animals/Pets
An Elephant Encounter

Allison Hickey   Other
Nautical

Clifford Sherman   People
Shoes Of A Painter

James R. Haarman   Nature
Kentucky In The Sky

Liliya Sitkovskaya   Other
Dolls

Margot Gallowitsch   Nature
Afternoon Diffraction

116

Ricky Wilburn   Nature
All-Seeing Eye

Joan MacFadyen   Children
Grandpa And Me

Kathleen M. Blake   Animals/Pets
Susie Sleeps On Her Back Often, Especially When Hot

Hourik Maadanjian   Nature
Nature's Reflection

Karen Rodenberger   Travel
Wyoming

Kathleen Doherty   Children
Untitled

Jeffery Lyles Other
Vancouver, USA, Fourth Of July

Ted Holland Animals/Pets
Nesting Mother

Laurie Apfelbeck Animals/Pets
Gunnar Gone Fishin'!

Marolyn D. Tipton Animals/Pets
Oh, Yum

Lisa A. Lidgard Nature
Relaxing On The Lake

Eduardo Oliver Nature
My House By The Lake

Sheryl McGrew Children
Where Are The Cherries?

Christina Morales Travel
Sydney

Alan DeDeaux Nature
Alpine Reflection

Carol Guthridge Nature
Last Of The Sunset

Linda Jason Animals/Pets
No Swimming

Tyler Whittall Children
My First Spaghetti Dinner

Noel Aralquez　　　　　　Nature
Sunrise In The Orient

Cathy Guyer　　　　　　Animals/Pets
Keeping Warm

John Bassett　　　　　　Nature
Mute Swan

Oren and Daphne Palni　　　　　　Travel
The Bellagio

William A. Rohan　　　　　　Nature
Bolts Of Light

Dennis Pawlowski　　　　　　Children
Wet Kisses

Cathy Ryerson   Nature
Ice Crystals On Sam's Window

Barbara Ann Racine   Animals/Pets
Resting For A Spell

Kathy M. Ryan   Animals/Pets
Fall Harvest

Lance Kannberg   Animals/Pets
Yearly Visitor

Barbara Schneider   Animals/Pets
Lion Cub Kisses Baby Goat!

Marian Boushley   Nature
Colorado Sunset

Nicole Doherty   Animals/Pets
Let Me In!

Marian L. Miller   Animals/Pets
Peek-A-Boo

Loretta Chavez   Children
Ashley's Tears

Sharon Casey   Children
Kent And Waldo Relaxing

Colomba D'Agostino   Nature
Cloudy Day On The Mountain

Linda Lokuta   Animals/Pets
Call Me Funny Looking, And I'll Eat You!

Dwayne Herndon Animals/Pets
Snuggle Foot

James R. Herb Nature
Fishing Buddy

Geraldine F. Austin People
Father And Son, Enjoying The Moment

Michael Paton Other
Hanging Lake

Delores Nieberlein Animals/Pets
Dezerray, Born To Be Wild

Joanne Boots Nature
Love On The Rocks

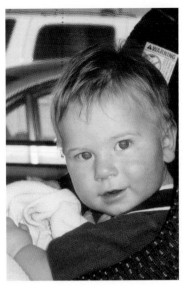

Linda Madison   Children
Ryan—Out Cruising

Anna Gorokhova   Children
I'm From The Renaissance

Patti Porter   Animals/Pets
Peeking Out

Erkentraud Magnuson   Children
A Very Special Christmas

Stacey Howlett   Children
Best Buddies

Carrie Green   Nature
Michigan's Morning Kiss

Paul W. Scheidt   Humor
Bad Hair Day

E. T. Lippert   Other
Moot Point

Julius Cinelli   Nature
Wilderness With A Human Touch

Lance Hamilton   Nature
Double Rainbow

Kaye Gosnell   Nature
Mountain Stream

Howard G. Jensen   Nature
Sunrise—Cedar Lake

Vona Williams　　　　　　　　Animals/Pets
Which Way Is Up?

Donna Fecto　　　　　　　　Nature
First Snow

Mary Kim Fitzgerald　　　　　　Children
Fall For Me

Maureen Butler　　　　　　　Children
A Child's Autumn

George Bussey　　　　　　　Other
Mill Creek Park Veteran's Memorial

Vonnie Kaylor　　　　　　　Animals/Pets
One Small Portion, Please?

Alexandra A. Hempel Sports
History In Progress

Linda E. Warner Children
Best Friends

Diana Lizotte People
Grandpa And Grandson In Umpqua River

Elizabeth F. Viau Humor
Friends In Leather

Valerie VanConnett Animals/Pets
White Buffalo Starting To Change Color

Julie Benson-Kiefer Animals/Pets
Ain't Love Grand!

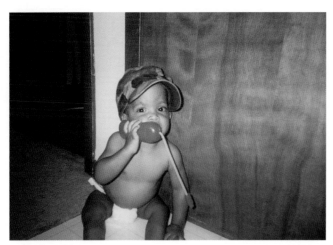

Kizzy Scott　　　　　　　　　Children
Top Secret

Gail Chanley　　　　　　　　　Nature
Dancing Light

Roy O'Berry Jr.　　　　　　　Humor
Fisted Fury

Sandra L. Herk　　　　　　　Children
Who's In My Garden?

Rebecca Hefner　　　　　　　Children
A Child's Love For Nature

Danica Martin　　　　　　　Animals/Pets
Sister Giving Brother A Hug

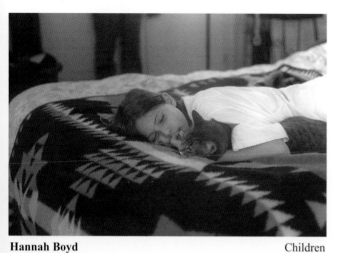

Hannah Boyd Children
Phoebe And Abby—Two Sleeping Beauties

Tony Free Nature
Newborn Fawn

Catharina Wolde-Yohannes Other
Serenity

Debbie Crockett Nature
Desert Hale-Bopp

Andrea Dean Nature
Fishing Spot

Carl L. Bush Children
Spider Baby

Eileen Donovan   People
Youthful Innocence

Ken Moreau II   Portraiture
Draped In Beauty

Kim Scarangello   Children
Terrible Twos—He Gets Into Everything

Adrienne T. Rosenberg   Children
Leo

Robin Jedele   Nature
Memories

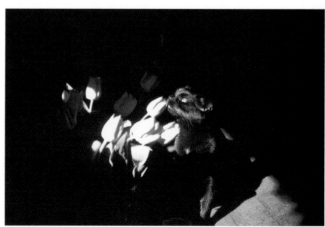

Robert A. Skripol   Animals/Pets
Abbie

Eleanor Bizzoso Nature
The Morning's Glory

Mary Anne Pilette Humor
Family Fun

Frances Johnson Nature
Abandoned Beauty

Mary Louise Yates Animals/Pets
Peek-A-Boo, Where Is My Lunch?

Betty A. Dart Nature
Horseshoe Falls, Munising, MI

Taryn Biggs Animals/Pets
I Knew He Was Good For Something, Buffy

Lynne Kuhn Animals/Pets
Getting The Kinks Out

Kathleen McGar Rooney Nature
Roses For Mother

Richard Rae Humor
Oodles Of (N)oodles

La Tonya Sanders Other
Ghetto Life

Deborah Ann Sanders Travel
Singapore Museum

Tom Reeves Animals/Pets
C'mon, Give Me That Chew Stick

Kathy Doughty   Nature
Butterfly Of Beauty

Jane Hollingsworth   Action
A Warm Place In The Field

H. C. McDaniel   Nature
Cades Cove, TN

Amanda Segovia   Animals/Pets
That's My Baby

Carrie Gliwa   Animals/Pets
Doggy Days

J. R. Drause   Travel
La Fontana

Joyce Evans Nature
Sunset In Mendocino

Marguerite Noah Children
Isn't It Nap Time Yet?

Laura B. Biery Nature
The Garden And The Gardener

J. J. Jackson Nature
Shadows And Snow

Alexander Macioce Nature
Yellow Mellow

Colleen Moriarty-Hinkle Nature
God's Watercolor

Virginia Roden   Nature
Rain In The Mountains

Cathy Longworth   Animals/Pets
Miami Metro Zoo

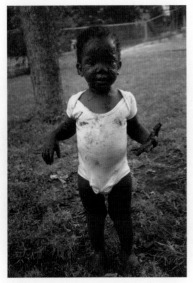

Derrick Johnson   Children
Muddy Baby

Michael L. Brown   People
Sand Beach

Frances M. Boehlke   Nature
Sunrise In The Fall

Ralph T. Schultz   Nature
Peace

Nicholle Leafblad   Animals/Pets
Let's Go

Opal M. Mitchell   Animals/Pets
Pansies, Beware!

Mary Ann Cline   Children
Precious To The World

Ellen Biggar   Animals/Pets
Roxy

Curtis J. Leach   Travel
Chicago

Linda Berry   People
My Grandson Playing

Wendy Jezowski — Animals/Pets
Kela Seeks Comfort From Her Favorite Toy, Little Man

David W. Lakin — Nature
Fly, Butterfly

Janet Lankford — Animals/Pets
Wait For Me

Katherine M. Dawson — Children
Pumpkin Patch

Lanettia Aldrich — Children
Reluctant Child

Laura Belarde — Nature
Reflections

Ruthann Graesser
Fall In Tennessee

Nature

C. L. Davies
The Race

Action

Willie J. Young
Peacock Bridge

Nature

Amy Thornton
The Forgotten City

Travel

Monique Cobbs
Berry 'N Ice

Nature

Lorraine Sturgeon
You Can Have It

Children

Patricia A. Bird   Animals/Pets
Cuddling

Jonathan Pelletier   Nature
Lagoon Reef

Robin Palmer   Nature
Fire In The Sky

Renee LeBlanc   Nature
To God Be The Glory!

Michele Miller   Nature
Almost Home

Scott Parsons   Animals/Pets
Bailey's First Fall

Teresa Bawcum   Children
Ready For Work

Elizabeth Nance   Nature
Reflective Confusion

Kevin Wittl   Other
Earth Moving Machine

Samantha Fortz   Children
Untitled

Bonnie Herbert   Travel
Whitby Abbey In England

Tina Flickinger   Nature
Sunset

Florence Hollingworth Nature
A Desert Storm

Chuck Lynch Animals/Pets
I'm A Lucky Dog

Matthew Bullock Children
No One To Play With

Travis E. Hartin Animals/Pets
Hard Day At Puppy Training School!

Kimberly Morrow Animals/Pets
Zeus In Hawaiian Shirt

Raymond Mansfield Travel
Urquhart Castle Ruins At Loch Ness, Scotland, Just Before Sunset

Ralph Kiertianis   Travel
Treasure Island

Marla Miller   Nature
Twin Lakes

Brian Reed   Animals/Pets
Rare Beauty

Nina G. Rudy   Other
Resting

Amy Roberts   Humor
I Think We Ate Too Much Birthday Cake!

Dorothy Allen   Animals/Pets
Playtime

Felix Margolin   Travel
Eiffel At Night

Bettye R. GrandPré   Other
Our Lady Of The Millennium

Robert B. Rice   Travel
A Diamond From Above

Rosemarie Hintze   Children
Waiting In A Window

Georgette M. Toews   Travel
Lobster Bake On The Coast Of Maine

June Brown   People
Sunset Over The Pacific

Ruth Anderson Animals/Pets
Take A Photo; It Lasts Longer

Judith Porter Nature
Dewdrops

Cynthia Thornton Children
Grandma's Little Heartthrob

Suzanne Proteau Nature
Serenity

Angela Guld Travel
Sultry Cancún Sunset

Mannie Samuels Travel
Hunting Island Light

Maria McAuliffe　　　　　　　　　　　　Travel
Sunset Over Province Town Harbor

Carol Briggs　　　　　　　　　　　　Animals/Pets
Ahh . . . What A Day!

Heather Marcus　　　　　　　　　　　　Travel
Flying High

Roland E. Wheeler　　　　　　　　　　　　Nature
Liberty Bell Mountain, Washington State

Ruth C. Norkus　　　　　　　　　　　　Nature
Morning Mist

Ed Marchese　　　　　　　　　　　　Travel
Romantic Venice

Shannon Pack   Animals/Pets
Quest For Freedom

Jeane M. Wolcott   Animals/Pets
Wha'da Ya Want?

Sandy Sagcal   Nature
Nature's Tranquility

Melissa Woodall   Nature
Diamond In The Rough

Rick Gabriel   Nature
Mirror, Mirror

Lori A. Pfingstler   Children
Jordan

146

Marcia Bodish   Travel
Key West Sunset At Mallory Square—Key West, FL

Angela Puckett   Animals/Pets
I See You

Karl Diehl   Children
Ocean Dance

Jody Moreland   Nature
Country Road

Bill Fisher   People
Praise The Lord

Adelia Hedden   Nature
Morning Silence

Mary L. Whitmer   Animals/Pets
Tummy Full Of Turkey

Betty Maybee Loyd   Nature
First Sunrise Of 2000—Pompano Beach, FL

Gita Shkiler   Portraiture
My Beloved Old Teacher

Tracy Pacovsky   Animals/Pets
I'm Sooo Sleepy

Kenneth W. Daugherty   Nature
Untitled

Jerry Crawford   Children
Pondering Life

John H. Phelps Jr.   Animals/Pets
Running With Shadow And Reflection

Gloria M. Musser   Nature
The Lord's Painting

Janet Continillo   Animals/Pets
Got It!

Brenda Sue Stone   Children
Ashley's Second Christmas

Lorraine McRae   Portraiture
Generations

Jennifer L. Swann   Children
Small Pleasure

Ryleigh Rose Smith   Nature
Reflection

Susan Helpap   Animals/Pets
Zeke, The Water Dog

Oscar Kilbourn   Animals/Pets
The Boys Are Having A Cool One

Anna Bebenek   People
Rainy Night

William L. Herron   Animals/Pets
Purr-fect Cat

Jennifer Driscoll   Animals/Pets
Contentment

Scott Ironfield Humor
Don't Even Think About It

Frances Jacobs Animals/Pets
The Lord Is My Shepherd . . .

Cindy Morse Nature
Time To Reflect

Stephanie Klassen Nature
Grandpa's Farm

Connie R. Stuckey Nature
Autumn In The Air

Joyce Hefner Animals/Pets
Hey, Where's My Chair?

Marie A. Armstrong Nature
Colorful Snowfall

Jennifer Leighton Children
Poppy's Flower Garden

Desi Calvert Nature
Following The Sunset

J. E. Zaher Children
What's That?

Beverly J. Sirgiannis Animals/Pets
Brrr, That Water Was Cold Today!

Robert and Susan Pilgrim Travel
Maui From The Ocean

Kim Williams   Animals/Pets
I Think I Can! I Think I Can! I Can!

Sandy Skeens   Nature
God's Creation

Edward J. Leroy   Animals/Pets
As Good As It Gets

Annette Kratka   Animals/Pets
The Cat Has The Couch!

Madleine Ruocco   Animals/Pets
Too Old To Argue . . . Let's Sleep Instead!

Clarence Walton   Humor
A Head Trip

Keri Skafas   Travel
The Smiling Test

Fran Stacey   Animals/Pets
Help! This Boat Is Taking On Water!

Jeannine Consigny-Williams   Animals/Pets
Sharing

Teri Wheeler   Animals/Pets
Sweetest Dreams

Sandy Nagy   Animals/Pets
Studious Lady

Maria Kritos   Animals/Pets
Sweet Slumber!

Elisha Friesen   Nature
Sunset Fire

Jack Schaefer   People
Grandpa And Granddaughter

Theresa Marie Luppowitz   Children
Smile, Here Comes Santa

Marija Fudge   Animals/Pets
Unconditional Love

Adolf J. Ehrl   Humor
Hitting The Sauce, I Mean Links

Alberta Bliss   Animals/Pets
Tigger Helping To Decorate

Eleanor A. Annis   Animals/Pets
When Will Santa Come?

Cynthia A. Stein   Nature
A Perfect Day

Holly L. Fabian   Nature
Just A Frog

Dolores M. Jackson   Animals/Pets
Angel In A Candy Bowl

Renee Kunkel   Animals/Pets
MVP

M. Magnifico   Animals/Pets
Caught In The Act

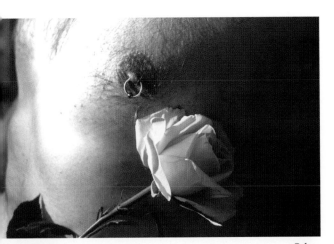

Patti Skeie Other
A Special Ring

James D. Thomas Nature
In All His Glory

Stephanie Ferrand Travel
Gateway To Heaven

Sandra Kay Wheeler Children
Sisters

Andrew Asherson Nature
Intensity From Above

Patsy Connelly Animals/Pets
Caught In The Act

W. E. Miller   Travel
The Forum—Rome, 2000

Dianne Scudder   Animals/Pets
The Girls

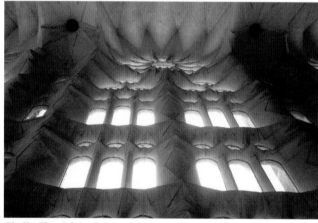

Shelly Hendricks   Travel
Inside La Sagrada Familia In Barcelona, Spain

Sarah C. Whittle   Animals/Pets
Lazy Daze

Glenn E. Rassi   Animals/Pets
Friends

Robin Cwalina   Humor
Can We Come Out To Play? We'll Be Good!

Samantha Baker   Nature
Walking Into The Unknown

Thyra Rathbun   People
Fresh Lobster Tonight

Margaret Champion   Nature
God's Fall Paintbrush

Michelle Hoffman   Animals/Pets
Old Friend

Herbert C. Boykin   Nature
The Search For Nectar

Jean Borrell   People
Freedom

Alex Allbaugh   Animals/Pets
Secrets

Michael Gebien   Children
Michael's First Christmas

Gwen H. Kjolso   Children
Oh, What A Beautiful World

Anita S. Miller   Travel
Niagara Falls, Canada

Candy Kenoyer   Children
Hard Day On Grandpa's Boat

Rachael McPhail   Animals/Pets
Fireplace Pooch

Florence Nelson Nature
Summer Day In Geneva Park

Sherry Lee Animals/Pets
Rifle And Lady

L. Nuray Alkan Animals/Pets
Life Shadow

Photographer Fisher Animals/Pets
Summer Beauty

Daniel Scherrer People
My Son

Robert Beatty Children
Sarah In Fall

Beverly L. Strickland   Animals/Pets
Bebe

Billy Irving   People
Untitled

Shirley Stange   Animals/Pets
What Do You Mean, Your Chair!

Clyde J. De Weese   Nature
Country Morning

William Thomas   Animals/Pets
Watching TV On My Waterbed, Enjoying The Waves

Michelle Wallace   Nature
Early Riser

Anita Von Himmel   Animals/Pets
Pals

Penny Spoutz   Travel
Once In A Lifetime

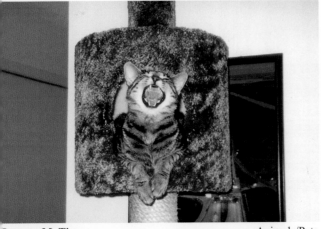

Lauren M. Tirone   Animals/Pets
Kylie Ends Another Long Day

Ann M. Myers   Travel
Evening By The Brooklyn Bridge

Rebecca Merritt   Animals/Pets
Zoo Pals

Ida B. Lyles   Nature
After The Storm

Alice Bromund — Animals/Pets
Surrogate Mommy Dog, Patches, Caring For Sunshine

Caroline Doughty — Children
Brynn

Debbie LaBella — Other
Horse Of Kentucky

Wesley L. Chu — Action
Nature's Calling! Praise God!

Patrice Nelson — Children
Mitchell On A Raft

Regina Miller — Travel
Na Pali Coastline

Mike Warren Humor
My Oldest Dog And My Youngest Daughter

Melody Mozes Animals/Pets
Houdini

Virginia Moore Nature
Nostalgia

Sheryl Batson Other
Shrimping At Sunset

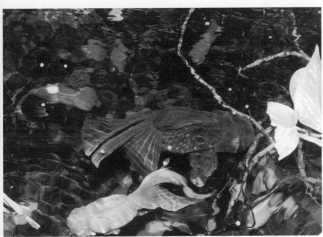

Linda Rohr Animals/Pets
Bubba And Friends

Jim Valenti Travel
Alcatraz Island

Cerissa Leah Johnson   Travel
Autumn Breeze

Sandra Janutolo   Animals/Pets
Fish Got Your Tongue?

Omie Godino   Nature
I Hope They Can't See Me!

Rosie Tenney   Nature
Chili Pinte Bush

Elfie Melvin McKinnis   Animals/Pets
Bunny Stew

Lois Weilert   Action
Fun In And Out Of The Water

Lois Babbitt   Animals/Pets
Nikki

Darby Root   Children
Sleeping Beauty!

Kristen Edwards   Nature
Tranquility Abounds In Nature

Kathleen Cooper   Nature
Colors Of The Fall

Michelle Miracle   Animals/Pets
Where's The Milk?

Virginia Mills   Nature
Memories

Stephanie Walters
Phoenix Rising
Nature

Vitaliy Boyko
All Aboard
Travel

Duncan McGinnis
I Know It Goes Somewhere
Children

James R. Fowler
Red Bird In Snow
Animals/Pets

Roxi Reeves
France
Travel

Shirley Brown
Saint Bernard Gracee Elan
Animals/Pets

Melanie Kuehl　　　　　　　　　　　　Children
Mandi, The Red-Nosed Reindeer

Ann S. MacMillan　　　　　　　　　　Children
A Serious Day At The Park

Mary Jane Gibson　　　　　　　　Animals/Pets
Another Spirit Freed

Greta Breiwick　　　　　　　　　　　Children
Alyssa Takes Over For Jesse In Toy Story II

M. L. Batchelor　　　　　　　　　　　Children
Rainy Day Train Ride

Cynthia Shaw　　　　　　　　　　Animals/Pets
Moses Begging

Christy Klobach   Animals/Pets
Bah Humbug

Nadya Petkova   Children
Baby Sarah

Brett Webb   Animals/Pets
New Little Brother

Scott Shelton   Nature
Winter Pine On Mount Mitchell

Mary Beth Aarns   Travel
Slovakians On Their Way To Church

Alicia Beck   Travel
Marines Raising The Flag At Iwo Jima

Clifford Brooks   Travel
A Journey Through Jerusalem

Marcellina Agostino   Animals/Pets
Shelly

Nick Franklin   Children
The Love Of My Life—My Grandson, Denis

Christine Stevenson   Sports
Rising To The Challenge

Kimberly Ball-Callander   Animals/Pets
Plum Tuckered Out

Marilyn Bruhl   Children
Granddaughter, Laura

Kathleen A. Lyons　　　　　　　　　　Children
A Boy, A Dog, And Summer

Betty L. Boyle　　　　　　　　　　Children
Reflections Of Christmas

Linda J. Hines　　　　　　　　　　Children
My Boys

Robert A. Lindsey　　　　　　　　　　Travel
Presidential Turmoil

Natalie Stroud　　　　　　　　　　Children
Listening To The Latest Gossip

Gloria L. Rodriguez　　　　　　　　　　Nature
Rising High

Susie Metz Grace Travel
Maui Moment

Robert Sheskey Nature
Swim Meet

Mary Miller Animals/Pets
The Lucky Seven Points

Mandy Lambert Children
Samantha Helping Daddy Wash The Car

Scott Abbott Nature
Appalachian Trail, Looking North Toward Mt. Washington

Mark S. Peniston Animals/Pets
A Squirrel At The Grand Canyon

Nancy J. Laughery People
A Freeze Frame Of Love

Michelle Garcia Children
A Day In The Hay

Marcella A. Glasgow Animals/Pets
Neptune's Folly

Elizabeth Cherniske Children
Little Pumpkin

Linda S. Jansen Other
History Still Stands

Joyce Miller People
Sisters At Sunrise

Norm Osborne   Nature
Reflections

Cynthia Hooks   Animals/Pets
Here I Am! Take My Picture!

Ahmed Ijaz Shah   Animals/Pets
Bison!

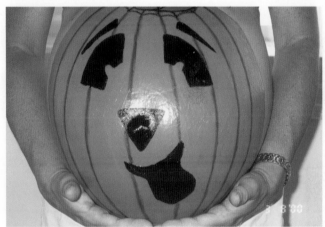

Carrie Peltzer   Other
Our Little Pumpkin

Lisa Flathmann   Nature
Paradise Below

Eydie Dickinson   Children
Tiny Bubbles In The Wind

Lori A. Watson   Animals/Pets
Taz

Louie H. Armenta   Travel
Newport, RI, Mansion

Megan Shepherd   Nature
God's Canvas

Elauna Antoine   Nature
Speechless In The Rockies

Janet Tamura   Other
Untitled

Lyn S. Perham   Animals/Pets
Backyard Visitors

James Bagnell   Other
Quincy Markets, Boston

Whitney Garland   Other
Santiago De Compostella

Robert H. Griffin   Nature
Nature's Fall Wonder

Missy Fendley   Children
Say Cheese

Betty M. Ruhlman   Children
Got Water?

James Nelson   Travel
Seaport, CT, Lighthouse

Terran McCollum　　　　　　　　　　Animals/Pets
Two Bums Up

Gay J. Williams　　　　　　　　　　Animals/Pets
Peek-A-Boo

Marian Bradford　　　　　　　　　　Travel
Walhalla—Gateway To Heaven

Milagros Escalante　　　　　　　　　Travel
Nature's Beauty

Jill Ann Price　　　　　　　　　　Animals/Pets
Sage

Megan Hurst　　　　　　　　　　Portraiture
Alter Ego

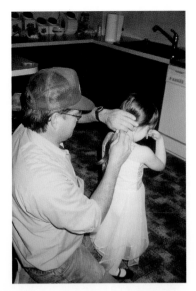

Monica Green People
Getting Ready For Dance Class

Dawn Phillips Children
Flying Birthday Cake

Rita W. Long Animals/Pets
Come Out, Come Out, Wherever You Are!

Mary K. Mohler People
Three Generations

Tricia Topping Animals/Pets
Romeo

William Hall People
The Green Goblin Is My Friend!

John J. Elko
Samba, Queen Of The Table

Animals/Pets

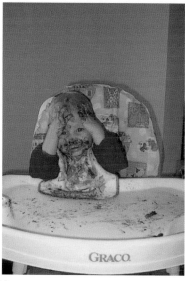

Eileen Beveridge
Mom Forgot The Milk

Children

Abe Monajjem
Yellowstone, 2000

Travel

Kim Brown
The Sweetest Kiss

Children

Ashley N. Nugen
Rain Forest

Nature

Ronald L. Pniewski
Me And My Shadow

Animals/Pets

Jeanne DeBlois　　　　　　　　　　　　Nature
Blazing Sunset In Maui

Brandon Castelletti　　　　　　　　　　Nature
Hummingbird

Vicki L. Walters　　　　　　　　　　Animals/Pets
Proud As A Peacock

Elaine J. Novak　　　　　　　　　　　Nature
Autumn At Shongum Lake

Cindy Drum　　　　　　　　　　　Animals/Pets
Two Hearts Grew Fawnd Of Each Other

L. Chris Durand　　　　　　　　　　　Other
The Rails

Garrett H. Frank   Other
Country Cooking

Terry Shannon   Humor
Where's Your Broom?

Adriana Torellini   Other
Nature Mort

Marcia L. DeFreitas   Nature
Night Blooming Cirrus

Karen Essner   Nature
Old Glory Weathers Another Storm

Sandy Radtke   Children
Snorkeling At Sunset

Barb Beck   Nature
Sunset In Door County

Marsha Robinson   Animals/Pets
Someday My Prince Will Come

Shirley Maze   Portraiture
New Baby Doll

Ed Kieffer   Nature
By The Bridge

Maggie Schrader   People
The Holiday Season On The Atlantic Ocean In Florida

Corliss Wright Alfred   Children
Rain And Leisure

Josh Marczewski Nature
Seven Sentinels

Ruth M. Coverdale Travel
Alaska

Marcella Drakulich Children
It's A Good Thing, Katie

Leslie M. Levenson Travel
Autumn Arizona Desert At Sunset

Linda R. Madson Humor
Butt Rock

Doris J. Brude Sports
Team Roping

George Gatt People
Honeymooners

Evelyn D. Smallwood Nature
Turning On Lights At Ambay Park Ball Field

Charmaine Cave Children
A Father's Love

Bobby Berry Animals/Pets
Muffin—Smiling And Sitting Pretty

Karyn D. Day Other
Moment Of Glory

Ashley Johnson Travel
Big Ben

Helen Vaughn   Nature
Sunset

Shirlene Ladd   Children
We Honor The Flag

Alexey A. Kalugin   Children
Twenty-First Century Style Of Cooking

France Allion   Nature
God's Cathedral

Mary E. Bergbower   People
Through The Eyes Of A Child

Sandra Post   Nature
Mother Nature At Her Best

Mary E. Steele   Animals/Pets
Unexpected Guest

Gretchen Barry   People
Choo Choo Has The New Big Shovel

Leo Peters   Humor
Don't Be Bucky

Dan Stafford   Animals/Pets
Laid-Back

Carla Graham   Children
Hello, Santa

Robert Hensel   Animals/Pets
Blackie, The Chipmunk

Robert K. Earl Nature
Into The Blue!

Lillian G. Smith Nature
Reflections Of God's Promises

Jennifer M. Duch Nature
Morning Has Broken

Jesse Tamez Children
Baby Ally

Theresa Drensek Nature
Dunes

Richard Stovicek Animals/Pets
Guard Dog

Irene Russell   Children
I Think I Can—Ali, Seven Months

Irving Boyle   Animals/Pets
True Love

Patty Hathaway   Animals/Pets
Beggin' For Attention

Anki Hill   Children
Best Friends

Cheryl Griswold   Nature
First Winter's Snow

Wendy Tatum   Animals/Pets
'Tis The Season

Julie Thompson   Children
Halloween Mummy With Spirits

Suzie Waldrip   Animals/Pets
Rusty's First Adventure

Jacqueline Leonhard   Children
Irish Boy

Anny Kraakmo   Nature
Interwoven—Sunshine And Snow

Tamara Livingston   Nature
My Haven

W. S. Adams   Children
Big Sister, The Protector—Little Sister, The Boss

Amber Testa Nature
Backyard Sunrise

Herschell Ted Chapman Nature
Sunset At Clark Hill

Allison French People
Grandpa And Me

Sean Oliver Action
Night Flight

Ethel M. Fender Animals/Pets
Bosom Buddies

Rafael R. Lopez Nature
Inspiration

Angela M. Schulle   People
What's She Thinking?

Donna Marucco   Animals/Pets
How Did I Get In Here!

Leeanne Schwartz   Animals/Pets
Beautiful Mother

Tami Wolfe   Animals/Pets
It's What Labs Do

Angela Gervato   Travel
Castle Used For Design In Walt Disney World

Patricia Gregory   Travel
The Peaks, Wyoming

Pamela C. Young   Nature
Babe In The Woods

Richard Schendel   Children
The Fourth Of July

Suzie Weis   Animals/Pets
Buddies

Chris A. Hernandez   Other
Winter's Echo

Shelley Trott   Animals/Pets
Real Rarities

Clara Everett   Other
Life Is Good

Winnie Goodin Other
Sunday Morn At The Millers'

Patricia M. Kenah Other
Home At Last

Geraldine Fernandez People
Ah, Venezia

Mary Ann Ellis Nature
Ducks Kissing The Sunset

Debra A. Sanderson Nature
Crystal Coast At Sunset

Shirley Mauney Animals/Pets
Snack Time

Marie T. Thomas   Animals/Pets
The Grass Is Always Greener

Walter Bond   Nature
Untitled

Kevin Reisz   People
Radiant Touch

Janet Cleveland Axtell   Travel
Pigeon Forge, TN

Richard C. Manville   Nature
Wickiup

Viola Ruelke Gommer   Travel
God's Promise

Susan Gronemeyer Animals/Pets
Stripe

Gretchen Slack People
Bad Hair Day

Connie Lynn Slay Children
Sweet Bubbles

Kathleen Brimhall People
Read To Your Child

Marlene Lewis Nature
Rainbow At Dusk

Carol J. Poland Nature
Stop And Smell Nature

Renee Schweikart   Animals/Pets
Na-Na-Na-Nah!

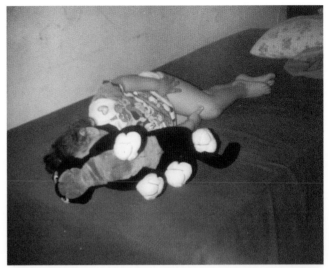

Vivian F. Fey   Children
You Can't Find Me

Barb Zodrow   Nature
Sunset In Orlando

Ulla Toikka   People
Hurry Up . . . It's Cold

Wilma O'Briant   Travel
The Fisherman

Hunter Jones   Animals/Pets
My First Snow Cone, Yum!

Lorraine Hahn — Animals/Pets
Sammy's New Hairdo

Rosielee Smith — Travel
Cruisin' On A Spring Day

Melody Thompson — Sports
A Shot In The Dark

Laura Free — Children
Great-Grandson Checking Out The Sales

Rose Buseck — Animals/Pets
How Do You Play This Thing?

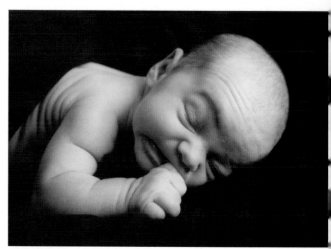

Lisa O'Neill — Humor
Elmer Fudd

Liz Joseph   People
Going Fishing

Robert R. Layton   Animals/Pets
Little Trucker

Karen Borger   Animals/Pets
Kena

Layne K. Strunk   Nature
Fiery Sunset

Evelyn R. Mashburn   Other
Leftovers

Robert Anderes   Children
Bottoms Up

Kim and Joey Simmons   Animals/Pets
Sleepy Time For Katie

Sue McClamroch   Children
Great-Grandmother Visits Brandon At Day Care

Linda Weimmer   Animals/Pets
Papa And Eber

Sandra Ard   Nature
Sunset Over Benton Harbor

Richard Arce   Humor
Two Sick Silly Putties

Linda M. Zanders   Nature
Missouri Reflections

Marilyn Mayse   Children
Nana's Little Man

Megan Keown   Animals/Pets
Undercover

Jasmine Williams   Children
Summer Love

Michelle Watkins   Animals/Pets
Uh-Oh, My Cat Broke

Rachel Starnes   Animals/Pets
Twins!

Jill Fink   Animals/Pets
Sitting Pretty

Fran Melega   Animals/Pets
Don't Fence Me In

Lisa Wallick   Travel
For Andrew

Debbie Hogan   Children
Can I Have A Bite?

Bonnie Jo Short   Nature
Transition

Christopher Sarra   Children
Goosh It

Dawne E. Ponsler   Animals/Pets
Portrait Of A Duck

Sally Reyes
Animals/Pets
Fall Wreath Cat

Amy Fender
Nature
The River Wild

Debbie Lee Carroll
People
Lizard Love

Michelle Loy
Animals/Pets
Mocha

Cindra Clark
Animals/Pets
Sundance Diablo

Sandra L. Oliver
Nature
Nature's Kaleidoscope

Grace Jean Fried   Nature
Iceland—Trolls' Work

Polly Beard   Animals/Pets
Waiting For Mom

Marcella Deitz   Humor
Where's Chucky Chipmunk?

Elena Bishop   Nature
Roses In The Snow

Cerine Jeanty   Other
Illusion

Brenda Reid   Children
A Day On The Farm

Amos Walls   Nature
Nature At Its Best

Michelle Hollis   Children
My Son, The Future Model, Starting School

Rebecca Gillen   Nature
The Ducks

Lisa Steiner   Children
The Boy And The Sea

Helen E. Brown   Nature
Autumn Glory

Rusty Hensley   Children
Child At Play

Jacque Anderson Children
Labor Of Love

Peggy Rekow Children
Taking Time To Stop And Smell The Flowers

Emmy Rackley Animals/Pets
Peek-A-Boo

Donna Kuehl Animals/Pets
Baby-Sitting

Lynn Childers Animals/Pets
Peek-A-Boo

Renate Schuler Animals/Pets
Black-Eared Dalmatian, Katja, In A Snowstorm

Magdalena Mikolajczyk   Travel
Changing Chicago

Hazel Irene Eatherton   Nature
The Unpredictable Hollyhock

Roy McDuffie   Other
What A View Of The Buildings

Dale Brennan   Travel
Sunrise—Kailua Bay, Hawaii, 1999

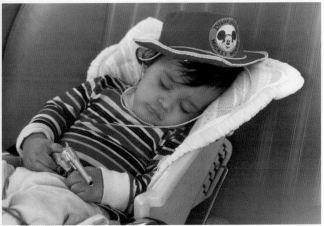

Doris Benedict   Children
A-rresting Lawman

Sherry Hornsby   Animals/Pets
Mego Eating Supper With Us

Jonathan Allender-Zivic   Nature
Rainbow In Disguise

Pennie Harpel   Nature
Untouched

Randy Hamrick   Travel
Dollywood

Erin E. Grover   Travel
New Orleans

Marjorie C. Crane   Children
Socked Out

Sandra D'Agati   Animals/Pets
Innocence

Julie Pasto   Animals/Pets
Here's Looking At You, Kid

Frances Dobishinsky   Humor
I Only Have Eyes For You

Ed DeAscentis   People
Caught By Accident

Mary Ann Wright   People
A Frown In The Midst Of A Newly Laid Foundation Festival

Julie Hocker   Animals/Pets
The Boys At The Beach

Becky Deamon   Nature
From Heaven To Hell

Nancy Fraser Children
Did You Say Something?

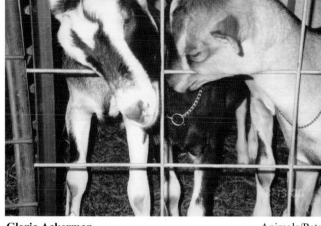

Gloria Ackerman Animals/Pets
Time-out Kid!

Steven W. Brennan Animals/Pets
Mickey

Millie Bailey Action
I'm Out Of Here

Mark P. Sevenich Other
Fall Election 2000

Geri Feehery Travel
Freedom

Viola Beltran   Children
Special Package

Laurna Laisdell   Children
Grandma's Angel

Pat Pentecost   Other
You're New Here

Lydia Pereira   Portraiture
A Flower Between Flowers

Jean Mefford   Children
Fairy At Twilight

Walter L. Head   Animals/Pets
What's Up, Duck!

Linda Provost　　　　　　　　　　Animals/Pets
Siblings

Rita Jankavich　　　　　　　　　　Humor
Henry

Nancy Holloway　　　　　　　　　　Animals/Pets
Let It Snow

Gail I. Burrows　　　　　　　　　　Nature
Two Rainbows

Beatrice A. King　　　　　　　　　　Animals/Pets
Free Spirit

Christine A. Coppage　　　　　　　　Animals/Pets
Sneaking Back In

Kathy Schaffer   Animals/Pets
New Kid On The Block

Becky Smith   Children
A Desire For Knowledge At One Year

Jeanette Dassow   Children
Bucket Of Love

Brenda Boykin   Nature
Beauty Beyond Fran

Barbara Ellen Lengyel   Nature
A Hand Painted By God

Chris Jarrard   Children
John Gets His Driver's License!

Kathleen V. Trout — Nature
Fall On The Old Farm

Cindy Wong — Children
No Peeking, Please

Ellen M. Means — Animals/Pets
Yum, Yum!

Debra M. Jones — Animals/Pets
Nap Time

Irene G. Brewster — Animals/Pets
Having Their Rest

Raquel S. O'Hara — Children
Johnny On The Spot

Bruce Albrecht Animals/Pets
Golden King

Deborah M. Webb Animals/Pets
Little Blue-Eyes

Julie Luoma Horpestad Nature
Sunrise Over Cape Darby, Alaska, With Dryfish Rack

Teri Lansberry Animals/Pets
Go Ahead, I Dare You!

Svea McAllister Animals/Pets
Rough Day At The Office

Paula Kokinda Travel
Sunset In Italy

Maureen Donovan   Nature
A Winter Sunset

Angela L. Johnson   Nature
Facing The Storm

Gina M. Dean   Children
Road Trip

Joyce Davis   Nature
Sunshine And Sea Breezes

Maureen E. Leonard   Children
Yummy Cookie

Julie Ann Miller   Travel
Serenity

Judy Wilson — Children
Holiday Warmth

Marjorie Boucher — People
Up, Up, And Away In My Beautiful Balloon

Mildred MacPherson — Children
Future Basketball Star

Clara Bosanic — Children
Sisters

Margaret C. Hicks — Animals/Pets
Stop And Smell The Roses

Marianne Kromkowski — Travel
First Train Ride

Brenda DeRossett Nature
The Sun Peeking After The Storm

Robert Woolley Animals/Pets
Man With Four Dogs

Ingrid E. Knight Children
Christmas Is Exhausting

Judith Hale Children
A Goldfish-Watching Day In Prineville, OR

Akehia Cheek Travel
Approaching Land

Carol Wakefield People
Barbecuing In The Rain

Joan Livingston
Bright Eyes

Children

Nancy C. Short
Boo! I Bet I Scared You!

Nature

Kathleen Bradley
Snow Flake And Santa's Best Friend

People

Don Moore
Tender Moments With Granddaddy And Granddaughter

People

Donald Short
Dr. Casey . . . Say Ahh

Children

Pattie Tracey-Schmidt
Moose In The Marsh

Animals/Pets

Bobbie Greenwood
Dare To Enter

Animals/Pets

Steve Roberson
This Old Tree

Nature

Susan J. Rose
Hide-And-Seek

Nature

Marlene Haselbauer
Kristina And Regalo

Children

Marlene Lewis
Mother's Helper

Animals/Pets

Stacey Patterson
From The Outside Looking In

Other

Christine Willner   Animals/Pets
She Loves Me; She Loves Me Not!

Angel Moraga   Nature
Heaven's Drawing

Deann Fischer   Children
Where're Your Shoes?

Sylvia Botha   Nature
Pupukeau Sunset

Priscilla A. Hills   Nature
Nature Has No Boundaries

Janet C. Frederiksen   Children
Sandpipers

Molly Wingerter   Action
Pen That Cow!

Shirley Dugger   Nature
Sky With Concrete Pillars In Driveway

Michelle Sutton   Nature
Gifts From God

Patricia Larimore   Action
Jet Waves

Maria Respicio   Humor
Baby Shark

Stanley D. Sloyer   Travel
Early Mormon Barn In Jackson Hole, WY

Louisa M. Gericke   Animals/Pets
His Lucky Day

Arthur V. Bennett   Nature
St. Peter's—Erie, PA

Angie Dudley   Animals/Pets
He Loves To Play Hide-And-Seek

Lynne M. Moore   Children
Everyone Needs Kisses

Shirley Miller   Animals/Pets
Patriotic Pup

Carlos A. Vasquez   Nature
The Hanging Lake

Lori Reynolds   Animals/Pets
Vegas Sideshow

Carmelinda Hotz   Animals/Pets
The Happy Gaucho From Argentina

Cindie Hilliard   Nature
Firestorm

Marie K. Swanholm   Nature
Freshly Fallen April Snow

Karen James   Travel
Lagoon Sunset

Kimberly Cromwell   Children
Good Morning, Sunshine

Anita Schockling   Nature
Room With A View

Julie Revollo   Nature
Backdrop

Marie Annette Creakman   Nature
Sunset In San Francisco

Kelly Hodges   Nature
Flowers

Edna Balce Sacro   Travel
Crossover

Sandra Harmon   Nature
Nature's Sanctuary

Helene Bushnell   Nature
Burned, But Still Thriving

Robbie George   Nature
Fickle Mother Nature

Kathy Hacker   Travel
Travel

William Burton   Children
A Boy And His Dog

Richard Leone   Travel
Maui's Treasure

Kari Freling   Nature
Mother's Flowers

226

Tracey Glasson   Animals/Pets
Rocky's Day Off

Tiffany Dreon   Travel
Two Harbors, Minnesota

Wanda J. Kriebel   Nature
Morning Glory

Andrew B. Balas   Children
Spackle Bucket Bath

Patsy C. Zimmerman   Travel
Street In Pompeii

Caz Mostowy   Humor
Mom's Laugh

Charles E. Sims   Nature
Sunset

Nola Manshp   Children
Grandma's Sunshine

James Otto   Animals/Pets
Odie Rides Shotgun

Daniel J. Berndt   Other
There's No Place Like Home

Leslie S. Mayer   People
Daddy's Little Girl

Laura Dierking   Children
Jake Dierking

Chari Emerson   People
Jason

Marge Drobenack   People
Lonely Streets

Debra Buckway   Animals/Pets
Unbearable Stress

Beatrice Jobe   Other
Raining Love On Our Honeymoon

Ron Haaksma   Nature
September Storm

Jim Stevens   Other
Double Rainbow Over Stone Church

Angie Bjorgan Nature
Lake Superior's Sun Catchers

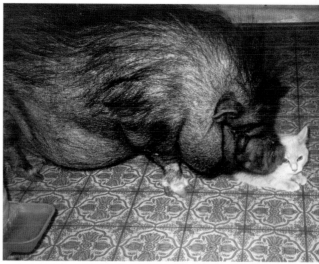

Allan Robbins Animals/Pets
Love At First Sight

Randi Walker Nature
Spider Snack

Alan L. Prutton Nature
Marco Island Sunset

William Kloosterman Nature
Majestic Power

Merle Williams Other
Uniquely Romantic

Roger Crispell   Nature
Two Swans Headed South

Robert M. Cosci   Nature
Meet Mr. Mushroom

Maggie Adorjan   Nature
Summer

Sandy Titus   Nature
Treasure

Rochelle R. Stroup   Travel
Sailing Away

Angela Wong   Children
A Time To Play

Sherrie L. Perry   Nature
Weekapaug Point, RI

Andrew Josheph Kowalchick   Nature
A Brief Shower

Christy Stull   Travel
Irish Sea

Sara Willis   Other
Dunagan's Store

LeAnne Peterson   People
Let's Play!

Diana McMakin Dodson   Travel
Sovereign Territory

KimberLee Snow　　　　　　　　　　　　Nature
Rose Blush

Melissa Saffer　　　　　　　　　　　　Nature
A Closer Look

Cyndi Blount　　　　　　　　　　Animals/Pets
On The Farm

Evelyn Kaylor　　　　　　　　　Animals/Pets
Plymouth Rock

Adam Uhrich　　　　　　　　　　　　　Other
Reflections

Edyta Kwasnik　　　　　　　　　　　　Other
Teapot

Patricia Anderson   Children
The Long Way Home

Karen Fletcher   Animals/Pets
Gotcha

Christopher B. Cline   Animals/Pets
What A Life!

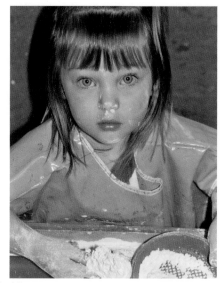

Crystal Smith   Children
Up To Our Elbows In Fun!

Jerry Cotten   Nature
My First Photo Of Lightning

Shelley A. Butler   Nature
After The Storm

Daniel L. Jones　　　　　　　　　　　　　　Nature
Yosemite Falls, 2000

Deborah Bleau　　　　　　　　　　　　　　People
Remembering When . . .

Karl Sprout　　　　　　　　　　　　　　Nature
Blackwater Falls, West Virginia, In October

Shirley McKay　　　　　　　　　　　　　　Children
Just Thomas

June Wiederhold　　　　　　　　　　　　　　Sports
Watching His Brother's Football Game

Amy Fries　　　　　　　　　　　　　　Travel
Bernoulli Fountain

Lorraine Accardi People
Fenway Fans

Margo Laugois Nature
Untitled

Adam Brown Nature
Wild Apples

Tracy Thompson Animals/Pets
Can I Please Go Outside?

Gina Bordeaux Nature
Bee-Ware

Nathan Erik Chaney Nature
Half Dome

Josie A. Campbell   Nature
Land And Sea

Gregg Kirchhoff   Other
Ali's Garage

Michael R. Carter   Nature
Abra Ham

Mert Johnson   Other
Sunset Silhouette

Bonnie Martin   Animals/Pets
Snack Time

Tina M. Pierson   Other
Echoes Of The Past

Doris J. Berger Nature
Basking In The Florida Sun

Charlotte Davis Animals/Pets
Amber Waves Of Grain

Gloria Willet Nature
A Bit Of Warmth In The Cold

Clara Wright Travel
Yosemite Falls

William Hames Travel
Hammerfest House

Katherine Mayer Humor
The Virgin

Shane Romagnoli Travel
The Franciscan Friary

Jordan Rushing Animals/Pets
Roaming Free

Louise Riles Travel
Manhattan From A Distance

Michele D. Gasper Other
As Darkness Descends

Timothy A. Greeley Nature
Icy Reflection

Jill Hoaglund Nature
Light Within

Jill Frost   Nature
Solitude

Robert C. Wilsford   Travel
Kintai Bridge At Iwakuni, Japan

Amy Riley   Animals/Pets
Just Hanging Around

Robert S. Charpentier   Other
Tugboats—Providence, RI

Joelyn Weston   Nature
Faces In The Clouds

Sarah A. Smrcina   Sports
Untitled

Evie May Guay   Nature
Autumn Tranquility

Jaclyn Bieniek   Other
Spiral Staircase Inside Florida Lighthouse

Ellis Pryce-Jones   Animals/Pets
Oscar Sends His Love

Linda P. Jones   Animals/Pets
Spoiled

Teresa Scarborough   Animals/Pets
Puppy Love

Vanice A. Lange   Nature
Autumn In New York

Sandy Ridgway   Animals/Pets
Lazy Afternoon

Gena Fite   Children
Closer Than Brothers

Louise Godbout   Nature
Storm In Progress

Jan Emming   Nature
Arizona Monsoon

Jessica M. Cruz   Travel
The Captivating Canyon

Kathi Nichols   Nature
Cove On Lake Cumberland

Joy Veland   Other
The Heavens And Earth

Sheila Knuth   Nature
Destiny

Gene Reighard   Nature
Sunset Over Nantahala Lake, North Carolina

Carolyn Como   Children
Amelia Feeding Seagulls

Corrie Clore   Nature
Crack Of Dawn

Mary J. Grefenstette   Nature
Twilight On The Beach

Lark Kidder   Children
Sister

Ken Dropek   Nature
Morning Tranquility

Betty J. Schick   Nature
Sunset Over Iowa

Josette Marie Gallegos   Nature
The Grand Tetons

Rhonda Estelle Garza   Other
Capture The Moment

Tracy Sanford Pillow   People
India

Jane Hamel   Other
Untitled

Carol Galligan   Portraiture
Veronica—Miss Apple Blossom, 1933

Eric Quimby   Travel
Rolling Toward Whitefish, MN

Leroy Matve Jr.   Nature
Fishing With Grandpa

Alice Krumwiede   Travel
D. H. Day Barn—Glenhaven, MI

Jon Mortenson   Nature
Aurora Borealis

Cruz Silva   People
The End Of A Soldier's Long Day

Lila Taylor   Travel
Shades Of The Past

Bobby Chin   Travel
Venetian Canal

Tina Holsclaw   Portraiture
Natural Beauty

John Tolbert   Action
Hydroblast

David Paschal   Nature
A Meeting Place

246

Michelle Chicks   Portraiture
Talofa!

Arliss Gorman   Children
Justin With Tears

Wendt Einfinger   Other
Reflections Of Yesterday

Gerald P. Ostrander   Nature
Bushkill Falls

Diana G. Dennis   Children
Barbecue Blues

Jack Sexton   Nature
Purple Onion Flower

Jolanta McNamara   Animals/Pets
Smokey Discovers Snow

Donna Joan Trippe   Nature
Mrs. Woodduck's Miracle Of Birth

Jennifer Yost   Animals/Pets
The Cat And The Clock

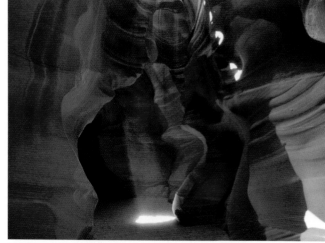

William Van Doren   Nature
Ray Of Light

Randy Kent Harvey   Nature
Springtime

Fred Stogsdill   Nature
Moving Stillness

Edna Pence   Other
Indian Mill, Ohio

Joaquina Bialer   Travel
Reflections

Holli Deal   Nature
Reflections

Christy Jacobs   Animals/Pets
Let's Play Ball

Tami Wyatt   Nature
Footprints In The Snow

Roberta Matthews   Children
Feels Good

Harriet Leach   Travel
Jaguar Sun

Rene Baker   Portraiture
A Precious Moment

Stacy Reeves   Children
Reflection Of Love

Aileen M. Garcia   Animals/Pets
A Pose Of Beauty

Nicole Blume   Animals/Pets
Turtle?

Timothy Allen Jenkins   Travel
Tybee Island Lighthouse

Betty Schneider
Mountain Sunrise

Nature

Penny Lee Skirvin
The End Of The Storm

Nature

Photographer Murphy
Sky Diver's Nightmare

Other

LaNiece Smith
The Messenger

Nature

Adam D. Lambrecht
Tree

Nature

Eugene C. Stevens
Sunrise Over The Wasatch Mountains

Nature

Nancy M. McFarland　　　　　　　　　　　Nature
Winter In Chicago

Kamala Slavonic　　　　　　　　　　　Children
Zoe

Annise Crame　　　　　　　　　　　Nature
Blue Ridge Waterfall

Craig Boutwell　　　　　　　　　　　Children
Who Are You Calling Pumpkin Head?

Sam Grilli　　　　　　　　　　　Nature
Bumblebee's Paradise

Cheryl Carter　　　　　　　　　　　Children
The Road Home

Milo P. Smith   People
Western Woman

Robin K. Nocks   Animals/Pets
Tasha

Julie Ann Allender   Travel
The Last Lighthouse

Katie Fry   Nature
The Pinks And Purples Of A Country Sunset

Lisa M. Stanley   Nature
Peaceful Waterfall

Doyce Miles   Children
Water Hose Drink

ARTISTS'
PROFILES

ACKERMAN, GLORIA
This photo was taken at the Westmoreland County Fair. I love animals, and these goats were especially cute. When my film came back, I noticed an extra pair of legs, and my thoughts were, "Just like people, these goats needed a little time to themselves." Thus, came the title, "Time-out Kid!"

ADAMS, W. S.
My family and friends are my favorite subjects. When I took this portrait of my daughters, I knew it was special. To be able to express my artistic abilities in this way is truly satisfying to me. I come from a very artistic family but never discovered my niche until after I had my third child at thirty-eight. I studied photography at home so I could be there for my children. Now I have a small business where I do portraits in people's homes. My goal is to always strive for quality, originality, and beauty in each photograph taken.

ADORJAN, MAGGIE
After taking photographs of the same things and the same people for thirty years, one needs to get a little creative. I tried to get a new perspective on a place we've visited many times. A small lake with plenty of shade makes this park a welcome relief in the middle of a hot summer.

AITKEN, BARBARA
I believe Monument Valley to be one of the truly unique places on Earth. No single photograph can capture the vastness and beauty, but my trusty point-and-shoot Minolta has preserved a small section of this incredible area. A twenty-by-thirty-inch enlargement hangs in my den to help relive this wonder-filled vacation and remind me that Mother Nature is by far the most skilled architect.

ALFRED, CORLISS WRIGHT
Every summer, my sister, Michelle, and her family drive down from Orlando, FL, to visit our parents in Baton Rouge, LA. My house is their rest stop ninety miles from Baton Rouge. The girls in the picture are Alex (the rider) and Kiri (the puller); they are first cousins. The rain started just as the girls got the wagon outside. I thought this was a cute moment as I watched them play uninterrupted even by the rain.

ALLEN, DOROTHY
This photo of Yoeshi and Yodah was taken with a disposable camera! On a nice fall day they were having their weekly playtime with their best buddies, Roxy and Maddie. Roxy and Maddie are my two dogs. The huskies like to run and hide together under the slide. It was a "Kodak moment!" Yoeshi is four, and Yodah is two. Yodah is from the humane society of Indianapolis, IN. Matt and Misti, good friends and neighbors of mine, are the huskies' owners. While they are working hard, I see to it that all the dogs get to play hard!

ALTLAND, BETTY J.
This is a photo of my kitten, Flicka. She is like a tortoise in color. She was three months old when this picture was taken. I took several pictures of her, and this one was my favorite. She loves to play and sleep on her amusement park. She also

likes to get up on my lap while I am on the computer and watch the screen. I also have a male Himalayan named Pharaoh. I am an animal-lover. I have raised toy poodles and Siamese cats in the past. I also love to take pictures of people, landscapes, and animals.

ANDERSON, LARRY
Wanting to explore previously unvisited fishing grounds, my boating buddy, Doc Lebow, and I towed my boat, *Sulinda*, from San Bernardino to Channel Island Harbor in Oxnard, CA, with plans to boat over to Anacapa Island. After arranging for a guest slip, we went in search of a market for provisions. When we reached the parking lot, I was amazed at the reflection in the calm harbor water, and I took the photo. I was more amazed after the film was developed.

ANDERSON, TINA
This photo was taken aboard a whale-watching boat near Fort Bragg, CA. It would not exist but for the good manners of a fellow passenger and photographer. He let me step in front of him, and he steadied me as I leaned over the railing step and hoped for the best. This lone gray whale dove at the very moment I pointed my camera. It was miraculous! I felt a connection with this whale, as one can only feel in their presence. Photography allows me to truly connect to the physical world.

ANTOINE, ELAUNA
Upon returning from my family reunion held in Glenwood Springs, CO, I was in awe as I glanced out my window at what I thought was one of the most beautiful sights I had ever seen! The way the mountains enclosed the water was so beautiful that words could not express the beauty my eyes beheld. I quickly grabbed my camera to freeze this wonderful moment, this wonderful time, the time I was "Speechless In The Rockies."

ARALQUEZ, NOEL
My wife, Clayr, and I were on vacation, and we took our two-year-old daughter, Nadchen Cyryll, to this beautiful beach for her first swimming lesson. The sunrise that I captured with my camera always reminds me of the wonders of creation and brings a mixed feeling of sadness and joy.

ARMSTRONG, MARIE A.
I was visiting relatives in early October, and while I was there it snowed. I went kicking in the woods. I looked at the river and saw the most beautiful scenery I had ever seen. The snow brought out the colors of the trees. It was a once-in-a-lifetime photo.

ASTBURY, CHRISSY
My parents were buying trees in a nursery in southern Indiana, and I was just fooling around with my camera. I never thought in a million years it would be published. Thanks! I was eleven years old when I took this picture in the summer of 2000. I used the new digital camera I bought with money I saved. I am now a sixth-grader at Zionsville Lower Middle School. My other hobbies include basketball, volleyball, and golf, and I play the flute and piccolo. I have an older brother, Thomas, and two cats, Fisher and

Tucker. My mom and dad are Dan and Kathy, and I have lots of friends in school.

AUSTIN, BETTY D.
The spring house in this photo stands in a little town outside of Florence, AL, called Cloverdale. I haven't been taking pictures very long as a hobby, but I enjoy taking pictures of old places, buildings, and more. I wish to become a famous photographer in the near future. I would like to add that I thank my sister for giving me the contest entry, and I would also like to thank my husband and family for believing in me.

AXTELL, CHRISTEL
Having grown up on Ripley Farms, a registered Guernsey farm in central New York, I have many pleasant memories of life in the country: the early morning quietness, the smell of freshly cut hay, the delight of a newborn calf . . . and the summer fun at the county and state fairs. Being close enough to home to carry on this tradition with my own children gives me great pleasure. At our state fair I was able to capture that moment of delight as our three-year-old daughter, Caylie, cuddled with a newborn calf. It brought back such fond memories.

BAGLEY, LEO
The family gathered at the homestead in Pennsylvania to celebrate Easter and the completion of renovations to the farmhouse built by our great-grandfather. We were especially pleased with the new, big country kitchen where we gathered around the big oak table that has been in the house for generations. Although we joked that Mom never wanted to change much in the house, the double rainbow was Mom and Dad's blessing from above to the family that, as she said, "You did good, and we're proud of all of you. Always remember how important family is and where you came from."

BAILEY, MILLIE
One of my hobbies is shooting wildlife with a camera. "I'm Out Of Here" was shot in my backyard with a manual-focusing 35mm Nikon using 400 speed film.

BAKER, SAMANTHA
I feel that life is a special thing and that nature is what fills us with the very life that is to be cherished forever. When I saw that life was imprinted into the Earth, I had to capture it for one reason—that a picture lasts longer! I want to thank my beloved for those very footsteps that made me want to capture life in action for a lifetime.

BALLINGER, MICHELE
This photo opportunity came from my own garden. I loved the color contrast, and the grasshopper acted as though he thought he was so inconspicuous. Nature is my favorite photographic subject. It's unique and offers infinite variety. I like nothing better than tramping through the woods with my camera over my shoulder. The trick is being there at the right time and always having your camera ready!

BARNES, LANETTE
This photograph was taken while our granddaugh-

ter, Kali, was spending time with us. We love Kali and wanted to preserve a moment with her. I believe this photo shows a child's natural reaction. Kali is our only granddaughter, and we cherish every moment with her. Friends and family label me Camera Lady because I carry a camera everywhere. I have been successful at a few local contests with animal photography. My favorite subjects of photographs are children, animals, and nature. They represent the innocence and beauty of life.

BARRY, GRETCHEN
Choo Choo is working in New Smyrna Beach, FL. He's on vacation with Grandpa Barry and Mom under the shade of the lifeguard station. He dug right in. He and his mom are from Colorado and love the sand and surf.

BATCHELOR, M. L.
Returning from a wonderful father-daughter vacation in the mountains of Georgia, my daughter, Ila, and I boarded the Amtrak train in Savannah for an exciting return home. While in Georgia, my childhood friend and hunting buddy, Walter Bryant, had given me a Minolta X-700 in need of repair. Guessing at the camera settings inside the dining car, I snapped a few photos. Returning to our seats, it began to rain. Ila turned to look out the train window; instantly, I focused and clicked, hoping to capture the moment. I think I did.

BEETLE, JULIE
I cannot begin to tell you how excited I am that you chose my picture for publication! I treated my husband to a hot air balloon ride for our fifth anniversary, and I took this picture as we sailed through the sky. It was a very breathtaking and serene experience. I have an eight-by-ten framed copy of this picture, which everyone who comes to my home loves.

BEIGH, MYRIAM
This image was taken in Door County, Wisconsin, a jewel of Lake Michigan. It was early one summer morning, and I was at the shore to photograph birds. I have been an avid amateur photographer most of my life. My son built a darkroom in my basement, and I do all of my own darkroom work. My favorite subjects are landscapes and wildlife. On this day, the gull flew right into the path of my camera, a vision of purity. It was like a gift.

BELTRAN, VIOLA
This is a photo of my eight-month-old grandson, Jose Alfredo Beltran Jr. His father is my son, Jose Alfredo, and his mommy is Maria, my daughter-in-law. Junior and his four-year-old sister, Lizbette, came to spend the day with their uncle, Cesar, aunt, Carolina, cousin, Tony, and me. Junior was attracted to the box as soon as he saw it. He fit perfectly. His smile told me he was delighted to sit in the colorful box.

BENEDICT, DORIS
Photography was an extensive fifty-year hobby of my late husband whose favorite subjects were children. I never learned to operate all his fancy cameras and lenses but was content to point and shoot my simple Contax T2. I took this picture of my grandson in the back seat of our car after a

wonderful day at the park. It is a big thrill for me to have his picture included in this book.

BENSON-KIEFER, JULIE
This is a picture of Katy (the tiger cat) and Motley (the white cat) enjoying the comfort of each other. They always lay around and napped together. This photo is more than a contest entry, but a lasting memory of Katy. This was the last picture of her before she was killed one month later. Not only Motley, but all of us miss her. . . . as stated by A. J. Fox, "A moment captured on film will live forever."

BERNDT, DANIEL J.
I don't know who lives there. I made a wrong turn and was somewhat lost when I saw it. Time seemed to stand still that fall afternoon in eastern Tennessee when I photographed the little log cabin. The smell of autumn leaves filled the air as I stood in silence at the edge of the dirt road. He loves nature, rocks for hours, warms by a fire, cares deeply, counts blessings, and never forgets that "There's No Place Like Home." I smiled as I drove away. I thought, "That describes the person who lives there."

BERRY, LINDA
I take a lot of pictures because I want to remember these moments forever. Shane Oliver is eight months old in this picture; his parents are Jeremy and Sonya Oliver. I am a single mom and Memaw—what my grandsons call me. I have two other grandsons, Rocky Skeen Jr. and Ashby Skeen. I have five daughters, so Shane has four aunts. They are Michelle Skeen (husband Rocky Skeen Sr.), Madonna Huacuja, Sue and Lyn Cockrell, Dorothy Oliver Clyde, and Opal Bundrick. We all live in or around Henderson, TX, except Melvin and Alberta Berry, great-grandparents; they live in Winnsboro, LA. We have a very close family.

BERTIAUX, LINDA L.
I was born and raised in Pennsylvania. I was on vacation in Pennsylvania, and I wanted to photograph an elk. I couldn't believe my luck when I saw the elk in a field as the sun was setting. I waited until the elk finished eating and starting walking across the field then stopped to be photographed!

BIALER, JOAQUINA
Two of my favorite things are photography and travel. I took this picture at the Delaware Water Gap Balloon Festival. When I saw the reflection of the balloon upon the water and the beautiful setting, I knew I had to capture that moment! I enjoy taking pictures of people, nature, and landscapes. Most of all, I enjoy taking pictures of my daughters, Chanamaria and Ysabela, who love to travel with my husband, Edward, and I.

BIENIEK, JACLYN
While vacationing in Florida, my parents and I visited one of the tallest lighthouses in the country. Together we climbed 203 steps up 175 feet to reach the top. While the outside view is spectacular, the spiral staircases inside are absolutely amazing. Looking down, I felt almost immobilized by fear, yet completely in awe of the breathtaking view from this unique vantage point. The

rising heat of the summer day added to the intensity of this dizzying, hypnotic, and truly mesmerizing sight. Although the staircases are separate, they create an illusion of one continuous, never-ending spiral that captures the imagination.

BIGGS, TARYN
I am a student at Blinn College in Bryan, TX. I am studying to be an elementary school teacher. I hope to teach kindergarten students. I sent this picture to ILP because it has two very special beings in it. The man is my fiancé, Jesse, and the dog is my eleven-year-old Pomeranian, Buffy. She and I have been together for eleven years. She is my world!

BIRD, PATRICIA A.
This is a photo of my Basenji, Keoni, and some of her puppies. I was surprised that I captured the puppies curled up in Keoni's neck with Keoni looking directly at the camera. With each litter, I hope there will be one terrific photo. This one is probably the best I've ever taken. It really captures how expressive Keoni is. I love my Basenjis.

BISHOP, ELENA
Snow came to west Texas in October this winter. It is rare for us to get snow before late December or early January. These humble roses withstood the cold temperatures and snow, plus the two following snows. It was such an unusual sight that I had to have a picture of the roses in the snow of 2000 to share with family and friends, because I knew they would not believe my story without a picture.

BIZZOSO, ELEANOR
Who knew that the morning glory seeds that I purchased for a fund-raising event would have blossomed so magnificently? You have to "catch" the early morning blossoms to truly appreciate their beauty. This photo is of one very special and glorious morning. I ran to get my camera to capture the angel's tears (dew) nourishing the flower. My father was a very creative and artistic floral designer and landscaper, and it is to his memory that I dedicate this photo.

BLACKMON, CHARLA
In November of 1994, my husband, Daniel, and I cruised the Nile River in Egypt, where I photographed and captured this breathtaking, glorious wonder of God on film, "The Sunset Over The Nile." It was truly an exhilarating and solemn moment in time and our lives—to reflect and remember our ancestors and to say thank you. The memories of our trip will live in our minds and hearts forever and in this photograph as well. Daniel and I have three sons: Mark, Darnell, and Alsalaam. We are natives of and reside in Oakland, CA.

BLAKE, KATHLEEN M.
I have always taken a lot of pictures, especially now that I have two grandchildren—Analyn, seven years old, and Thomas, fifteen months old. I also have many of Susie and my cat, Summer, along with other family members and parties. I bought Susie at a shelter in Spokane, WA. I wanted a Chihuahua, so I went to a shelter where they had a Chihuahua and Pomeranian mix. My cousin was with me, and she said I didn't want any part

of this, as we had two other dogs at home. I had to have this dog. I fell in love with her right off the bat. She weighed three pounds and had no hair. I told my cousin I was going to name her Susan, and she said to call her Susie. I brought her home. Everyone fell in love with her, and she fell in love with everyone except the mailman. Susie is now nine years old and has lots of hair. Summer is my cat and is fifteen years old. I live in Arcadia, CA.

BLATSTEIN, PERRY
This picture was taken at Camp Nock-A-Mixon, where I go for seven weeks of the summer. My picture is unique because it includes a few counselors playing in a color war game. I would like to thank the athletes in this picture for making it as good as it is. Another thanks goes to all my summer friends for making me want to come back every year and take more and more pictures!

BLISS, ALBERTA
Tigger is the son of a cat that came to our front door ten years ago. She was nearly starved to death, but we nursed her back to good health. Tigger was one of five babies she soon had. Our grandson quickly claimed him; Tigger would have to stay on the farm with us. He has always been very intelligent and very interested in Christmas, especially the decorating. He quickly goes under the Christmas tree to make his bed. He seems to realize just how important Christmas is.

BOEGE, DENISE
A long-time friend invited me to go to Niagara Falls to attend her granddaughter's graduation. I had never been to New York and was excited to see Niagara Falls. There were so many beautiful places surrounding the park, but this place was so peaceful. I sat there and enjoyed watching and listening to the water running over the rocks, and I was glad I could preserve the image on film.

BOEHLKE, FRANCES M.
I'm a fifty-eight-year-old wife, a mother, and a grandmother, and in the year 2000 I became a great-grandmother. I purchased my good camera about five years ago and have been snapping pictures ever since. I was standing at the sink putting my coffee pot together when I looked out the window. There was the picture "Sunrise In The Fall." It was beautiful, more beautiful than the picture. I love taking nature pictures. My husband is now retired, and so am I. I worked at the high school in the kitchen.

BOOKER, THERESA
This precious moment was captured while I was working at home on my computer. My nephew, Dae'Shun, and my dog, Bambi, wanted to go out and play; however, because I had work to do, I could not take them out. Dae'Shun walked over to the window and knelt down, looking out the window, which overlooks the pool, swings, and slides. Bambi walked over and sat beside him. Dae'Shun reached over and put his arm around her, and together they wished in silence to go outside. It was so special that I quietly retrieved my camera to capture the moment. I showed this picture of "Best Friends Wishing" to my husband,

Patrick. He wrote a poem that captured this moment perfectly.

BOOTS, JOANNE
This is a photo of painted rocks at the Hi-Tide Resort in Moclips, WA. My husband, Toney, and I try to get to the beach on our anniversary every year, and we always paint a rock to celebrate our love. I take my camera everywhere, and my favorite place to photograph is the ocean. It has so much meaning, and the beauty holds a special place in my heart.

BORRELL, JEAN
Of all the pictures I have taken over the years, this one of Moira, my twenty-year-old granddaughter, is the best. "Freedom" is expressed on her three-wheel bicycle to get around town. She was born with Down's syndrome, and because she had special needs, her loving parents worked diligently to get her the best education they could. She has three brothers, loves all sports, and plays basketball. She was on her way to watch a football game on TV at her cousin's home when I snapped this picture. Moira will graduate from high school this spring 2001.

BOTHA, SYLVIA
After relocating from South Africa to Hawaii, I have been fascinated with the exquisite, ever-changing sunsets on the islands. This particular photograph was taken from our lanai one afternoon as we sat admiring nature's awesome beauty.

BOYKIN, BRENDA
This photograph was one of many taken on our annual camping trip down the Tar River. But this particular photograph was taken just after the destruction of Hurricane Fran in 1996. We were expecting that we would see lots of destruction, but much to our surprise, just in the middle of all the devastation after the hurricane, there was still all this beauty.

BOYLE, BETTY L.
Christmas has always been a fun time in the Boyle household, even more so now with grandchildren. On this particular Christmas night, Nelda gave us all the meaning of Christmas in one picture. I have always enjoyed photography and sharing prints with family, friends, and coworkers, many times in the form of postcards with titles. It is fun and challenging attempting to capture the perfect sunset shot or people and animal antiques shot. Our daughter and her husband have blessed Lewis and me with a grandson who provides me practice with action shots during baseball and soccer seasons.

BOZANT, ROBERT
While my wife, one-year-old daughter, and I were outside our home watching a storm come through, I was able to take this very lucky shot of lightning that posed for us. It's not every day that an amateur like myself is able to capture such a beautiful piece of nature.

BRENNAN, STEVEN W.
Mickey is a wonderful cocker spaniel rescued by our local humane society. We adopted Mickey after walking dogs one Sunday for the humane

society. Mickey lives with cats and a rabbit that came to us either as strays or from animal rescue groups. This photo was taken on an extremely hot summer day when Mickey was excavating a cool cave in a shady spot. We would like to encourage everyone to adopt a stray from their local humane society or animal rescue group and to spay and neuter all of their pets so that all animals will have a loving home.

BRIGGS, CAROL
Ashlee Rae is my first kitten, and I have enjoyed taking many pictures of this comical, ever-changing pet. However, photo shoots can be exhausting. I just happened to have the camera ready when Ashlee communicated that this would be her last photo for the day.

BRIMHALL, KATHLEEN
This photo expresses the love and devotion of a father for his child and how this special closeness comes through with the reading of a bedtime story. It is the beginning of a life-long love of learning, the greatest gift of all. None of this was staged—not the lighting, the positioning, or even the bunny rabbit looking on. Catching this photo moment was priceless.

BROOKS, STONEY
Seascapes are one of my favorite subjects, especially when they have that ethereal quality. On days like this one, the mist and the waves, together with the setting sun painting the clouds, invoke a sense of dreamy contemplation, transporting one's imagination across space and time.

BROWN, HELEN E.
Autumn in New England is a very beautiful time of the year. The village where I live is especially beautiful, and our pond reflects the foliage in all its glory.

BROWN, JUNE
I have been a photographic enthusiast for many years. Living in Southern California, I had the opportunity to witness and capture on film some of the most breathtaking and inspiring scenery to be found possibly anywhere in the world. "Sunset Over The Pacific" was shot on a warm summer evening from a sandy beach in San Diego. I'm honored and privileged to share this treasure with everyone. I hope your enjoyment will be as great as mine.

BROWN, MICHAEL L.
I started taking pictures a couple of years ago, many just of family and friends on special occasions like birthdays and holidays. Now people have seen my pictures, so I've been asked to do anniversary parties, weddings, and senior pictures. Now people I do not even know are calling me to take pictures for them.

BROWN, SHIRLEY
This photo is of Gracee at Swan Creek in Gallatin Canyon, Montana. The fall colors made a beautiful background setting for our pet, Gracee. We bought her from breeder Kathy Gerving. Her dad is Yurraman Jundah, and her mom is Anab's Queen Jezebel. Our granddaughter, Ashlee, my husband, and I attend Lisa's obedience class every

week. What great fun we have. I don't take pictures often, but this photo just captured an image of the warm day, beautiful fall colors, and our Gracee that we can look back on forever.

BROWNING, RICKY LEE
Alaska's wilderness is as beautiful as its people. When I go fishing, I take my dog, Ben, Little Bear. Four-and-a-half miles out of Palmer, AK, you'll come across Moose Creek. A mile-and-a-quarter upstream there is a waterfall that is fifteen feet tall. As I walked downstream a little, I noticed my dog lying by a big rock. My dog doesn't like to be photographed, so I had to take the photo fast. Ben's mother's name was Mishka. Mishka in Russian means "little bear." My dog, Ben, tries to catch salmon. Sometimes he succeeds, and sometimes he doesn't. He learned it from his mother, Mishka. That's when I gave my dog, Ben, a nickname—Little Bear.

BRUDE, DORIS J.
My two sons and my daughter have become amateur team ropers, and they enjoy the sport so much. My son Brian sent his buckskin horse, Skip, to a ranch in South Dakota to be trained for team roping. I snapped this picture showing Skip's new roping skills when we went to the ranch to bring him home. This is a great sport, which is gaining a lot of popularity in our state. It's a true team effort.

BRUNELLE, JOAN M.
Forty years ago, I bought a book about twelfth century cathedrals. The Abby Church was the front plate of the book. It began a lifelong dream to see the mount. Last September, I was in Normandy on Elderhostel to visit WWII beaches. We took a side trip to see St. Michael's. I was finally able to climb the mount to the Abby Church. It was a dream come true!

BUGIEDA, CHERYL
On a beautiful summer day last August, while recovering from surgery, my father decided to take me out. Grabbing Mom, but not before grabbing my cameras, we headed out to a nearby shopping center and an area park, which is a haven for ducks and geese. I went through a roll-and-a-half of film, but of all the pictures, this is my favorite. I love to take pictures of all kinds of things, but I think photographing nature is my favorite. I enjoy taking walks and snapping shots of stormy skies, the clouds over the river on a clear summer day, and little families of ducks on outings together!

BURKHART, SARA E.
The power of water is so incredible. This photo was taken at Mammoth Springs, Arkansas. I was standing on the bridge over the spillway and was so amazed at the beauty and strength of the water. I leaned over the edge and took the picture. Wow, what an amazing perception of the spillway. Mammoth Springs is a very beautiful place.

BUSHNELL, HELENE
This photograph of the Grand Mineral Pool was taken in Yellowstone National Park. My boyfriend, Don, and I had seen it at eye level with the other tourists, but we decided we needed a better view. We climbed up quite a large hill

behind the pool and promised not to look until we got to the top. We reached the highest point and turned around; it was the most spectacular sight I had ever seen in my life. Looking through my camera at this wonder and others like it in Yellowstone that summer is what made me want to be a photographer.

BUSS, SHAWN
I have always enjoyed trying to capture some of nature's beauty on film, and this photo captures some of Peyote Canyon's. I remember making the mile-long climb and asking folks coming down, "Is it worth the climb?" It was well worth the climb! The view was breathtaking, and it is most gratifying to share that beauty in this publication.

BUSSEY, GEORGE
This is a photo of the memorial that was dedicated on November 12, 2000, to all veterans. It's located in Mill Creek Park in Willingboro, NJ. This is the first of this type of monument ever like this built in Willingboro. I believe it is one of most beautiful ones in Burlington County. I took this picture because it has all of the armed services flags represented. I try to have my camera with me at all times because a moment captured on film will live forever. This is the first time for me to have a photo entry in a contest ever.

BUTLER, SHELLEY A.
It was very windy that morning. The clouds broke up and blew away after lunch. Returning from our day hike, we happened on this view of Lake Superior. I love being out in the woods and photographing nature in all its splendor.

BUTTERFIELD, JAMES
A collar-guard kept Megan from scratching her infected ear. It was the only time this treasured member of our family was visibly saddened.

CABANISS, LINDA
My granddaughter, Brittany, and I had gotten some mail out of my mailbox, and she looked back and saw our precious cat, Lexie, pulling one of her many antics. Brittany ran for the camera, and we got this once-in-a-lifetime shot. I take pictures of my cats often, but this one was the topper! I live near my daughter and family in Saluda, SC. I have two wonderful grandkids and four precious cats to always make my day brighter. With Brittany, Zach, and my pets, I am blessed indeed.

CANNELLA, JANICE N.
Motorcycles have become a real passion for me. The sights I see and can photograph from the back of a Harley are phenomenal—the kind of panoramic views that can be lost in an enclosed vehicle. This photo was taken on the return of a two-thousand-mile trip. With the wind in our faces and the sun setting to the west of us, I looked down and saw our shadow on the highway. I felt it depicted the feelings of incredible freedom I always get when we ride.

CARLSON, KATHLEEN J.
We were going to Bremerton, WA, and the fog was thick. The ship was barely visible, yet very ghostly looking. I find Mother Nature a fabulous

artist, and I'm extremely lucky to get such interesting pictures. I take my camera everywhere.

CARROLL, DEBBIE LEE
I carry my camera with me one hundred percent of the time because you never know when a moment like this will pop up. Although I was never a reptile-lover, I fell in love with this man, Jack, and his lizard, Stanley. We were having coffee at the kitchen table, I looked up, and there were my boys.

CART, DANA
This is a photo of my son, Jonathan, shooting his first arrow during archery at Cub Scout day camp. I came not only to volunteer as a den mom, but also to take pictures of Jonathan for his scout scrapbook. As a creative memories consultant for five years, chronicling my family's life through pictures and journalizing is very important to me. Taking photographs has been a hobby of mine for over twenty years, and I've had the same Minolta camera since 1982. Yet capturing this "Arrow In Flight" was pure chance and not skill. That's what makes life and picture-taking beautiful.

CARTER, CHERYL
This is a photo of my grandson, Kain, at our last family reunion in Wyoming. I have always had an interest in photography, and I keep a loaded camera close at hand. When we look at our photos of the past and present, we are reminded of the beauty and joy that life represents. We find "The Road Home" easier and more enjoyable.

CAVE, CHARMAINE
Never in my wildest dreams would I have thought that my photo would be published! What an honor. We were on vacation when I took this picture of my husband, Marlon, and my son, Jacob. We were waiting for my cousin's wedding to start, and my son just conked out. When I took the picture, I did not comprehend the effect the picture would have. It was not until it was developed that I realized, "Wow, what a great picture." I kept this photo in my private stash of special pictures that I look at when things get me down during the day. Looking at these pictures always puts a smile on my face and makes me forever grateful for my family. I was showing a friend these pictures when she suggested that I send a submission. The rest is history.

CHENG, C. C.
I started taking pictures at age eight, when my aunt gave me a box camera. After retirement from the University of Kansas Medical Center, my wife, Katherine, and I moved to Delaware in 1998 to be near our oldest daughter's family. A house-warming gift from our youngest daughter, Audrey, was a bird feeder, which we hung outside the breakfast room window. Every morning, little birds come by enjoying what we've provided. This picture is a record of one of these happy occasions.

CHU, WESLEY L.
I went to the New York Hall of Science in Queens, NY, for an exhibition on the wonderful world of reptiles and was inspired to shoot this photo. It means our dear God has created nature for us boys and girls to have fun in and share with one anoth-

er. Brooklyn, NY, is my home. My auntie Anne shares many precious times with me in different games. She gave me my very own camera to shoot pictures with for my ninth birthday. I thank dear God for it!

CINELLI, JULIUS

My fiancée and I were on a vacation at a fishing resort in Canada. Needless to say, Canada is a wilderness country—except we seemed to make a friend of this little chipmunk. We were both amazed at how friendly he really was, as you can see. He actually made our whole vacation, and we'll cherish those moments forever.

CLARK, CINDRA

Fire in the sky. . . . fire in the eye. An Iowa sunset with "Sundance Diablo." More aptly named a cat will never be. From humble beginnings in a Florida fisherman's shack to the wide open spaces of the great Midwest, our shabby tabby has traveled afar with a big attitude and a bigger heart. From a golden beach bum, to the "great field mouse hunter," Sundance has filled a void in our childless lives, becoming our loving but mischievous Sunny Devil!

CLAY, LISA

This is a photo of one of my four cats—Hacoona. I adopted Hacoona from the Monmouth County SPCA of New Jersey in April of 1995. While Hacoona gazes out on the blizzard of '96, I can only believe she is thinking that she is glad to be inside—warm, fed, safe, and loved. Although she had a very rough start to her life, she is a very affectionate and loving cat. To me, she is one of many angels purring on Earth.

CLINE, MARY ANN

This world would be such a sad place without children. My husband and I have been blessed to have such a wonderful little boy. He has brightened our lives and filled our hearts with joy and love. I thank God every day for my child. Children are just precious to the world.

CLORE, CORRIE

I am a seventy-nine-year-old widow with muscular degeneration in both eyes since 1997, who enjoys the beauty of nature. I took this photo with a twenty-seven-year-old Vivitar 600 camera on Kodak 110 film. I bought it for a trip to Holland to see where my mom and dad were born. They first met each other on the ship to America in 1912. My Vivitar 600 Instamatic has been with me on all my trips since 1974, so it was thirteen dollars well spent. It's so handy to carry in my purse to capture that right moment.

COATES, DEBORAH

I am a designer by profession and an artist by nature. Photography is a fun way to capture God's palette, canvas, and creativity. "Wagner Falls" was one of the many gorgeous waterfalls we experienced on a four-day adventure of the Upper Peninsula of Michigan with my newlywed husband, Russ, and our dear friends, Bill and Patty. I love to paint and create. Now, I've found that photography can be a fun, easy way to experiment in a creative medium wherever I am.

COLE, ZELA

I have loved photography all my adult life. I am a seventy-one-year-old housewife and grandmother of four. Fall is my favorite time of the year. I always take a lot of photographs, and in winter I love to take photos of snow-covered trees and mountains. I am a native West Virginian. I come from a family of eleven children.

COLLINS, JIMMY

On a summer night in August, Luke Dobbyn, my grandson, was with the rest of the family at the ballpark in Arlington. Luke looks as though he is looking at the flag during the national anthem, when in reality he was watching sky divers jumping into the ballpark during the opening ceremonies. They definitely attracted Luke's attention!

CONSIGNY-WILLIAMS, JEANNINE

Believe it or not, Tate and Coby are from the same litter. In this photo, they are about four months old. We call them our twins, even though they look nothing alike. Oftentimes, they will be chewing on the same toy, either a nylon ring or rag toy, as in the photo. Making pictures with them is really a challenge because they aren't often still. Photography is one of my hobbies, and these rascals have given me plenty of material to shoot.

COSTANTINO, RANDY

"Microscopes" was taken at a lake near my home in Prescott, AZ. The children were hunting crawdads and were so intent on their adventure that I was able to slip up and shoot a few frames. This photograph is typical of my style and strives to show the viewer how extraordinary our ordinary world is.

COUCH, SANDRA

I enjoy photographing my four cats demonstrating their "human" actions. They were being toilet trained, and no one believed this event! So I sneaked a photo of Kemosabe during her private moment as proof that my cats are trainable and human-like. All four have this intimate moment on photo now! They also watch TV, play ball, get their teeth brushed, eat angel food cake, take vitamins, and see their doctor yearly for physicals. T. C., Tiger, and Spooky now await their turns to be nationally recognized in the future photo contests. Each has their own special talents to show.

CRAME, ANNISE

This a picture of the most majestic and beautiful creation of Mother Nature, a waterfall. The Blue Ridge Parkway is full of many beautiful scenes like this one. This is a vacation that should not be missed by anyone. A trip on the Blue Ridge Parkway is an experience that you will never forget.

CREAKMAN, MARIE ANNETTE

My friend, Dan, was visiting me from Vermont. We had driven to San Francisco from Los Angeles to explore the Haight-Ashbury district of the city and, of course, the Golden Gate Bridge and Alcatraz. Torrential rain poured all day until late afternoon when the sky suddenly cleared. We rushed to the beach and made it just in time to experience this beautiful gift of a sunset.

CRISPELL, ROGER

Ann, my wife, spotted this photo, taken from our balcony, which overlooks a small lake. The swans are among the guests that we enjoy for several days every spring and fall, as they migrate north and south. I am a retired design executive with a camera always nearby. Photography has been an important part of my entire adult life. I was happy to add the swans to my collection of prized photos.

CROCKETT, DEBBIE

I spent many nights enjoying Hale-Bopp in the night sky. I wanted to be able to remember it with a picture of my own. My husband, Joel, and my children, Victoria and Dustin, encouraged me to submit this picture.

CROTEAU, RONALD

It was a misty day when I shot this view from the side of a hill. I had to balance the camera with one hand while I held back brush with the other hand. The mine is located two hundred miles east of Anchorage, in a remote site of the Wrangell Mountains. I spent ten years in Alaska, and as a hobby I had the good fortune to explore and photograph many of the state's great wonders.

CUNNINGHAM, JOANNE

We got Dozer when he was four months old. He was part Lab and part German shepherd. Every Christmas, we would buy him a gift of rawhide toys and hang them upon the doorknob. He would find them and tear them apart. As you can see in this picture of "Dozer With His Lollipop," he had that look of amazement. Since it was Christmas, I already had the camera out to snap this picture. Dozer was a very smart dog. There were a lot of tricks he did on his own. Here are a few: he would fetch my slippers every night at the same time; he would say "I love you" in doggy language; he would give you a hug with his paws around your neck; he'd get the newspaper and would even steal our neighbor's; and he'd open cabinets to get his biscuits. The best thing of all was that he loved us, and we loved him. He gave us so much joy in the thirteen years we had him. He is no longer with us. He had cancer, and we had to put him to sleep. He will always be in our hearts.

D'AGATI, SANDRA

This photo was taken three days after this stray puppy was given to me. She was about twelve weeks old when I took this lucky shot. Winston has outgrown most of her shyness. She loves people and enjoys playing with other dogs. I look forward to the many years of enjoyment and entertainment that Winston will provide.

DABOUL, KATHY

I'm a serious amateur photographer who loves to take pictures of nature and people. As an avid artist and crafter, I am always seeking new ways to express my creativity and vision through photography. Largely self-taught, I enjoy practicing and mixing my various hobbies and sharing the results with my family and friends.

DAIGLE, LUCILLE

I love to take pictures of my kids. As soon as they see the camera they usually stop and pose for me out of habit. When I looked out the window at my daughter, Laura, I couldn't resist snapping this candid photo. It was her fifth birthday and a picture-perfect day for picking flowers. Laura looked so peaceful and lost in thought in her "Field Of Dreams."

DARABI, PARVIN
I grew up in an Islamic culture where art is not considered important and where many artists are imprisoned or even persecuted for their artistic expressions. As a girl, I wanted to play the violin, but I was denied because "good girls don't become motrebs (a derogatory term describing musicians)." This type of thinking killed all my artistic aspiration as a child. For the first fifty years of my life, I thought I had no talent for art. Recently, I decided to take photography, and the picture "Mother And Child" is one of my first few pictures.

DE WEESE, CLYDE J.
My granddaughter, Audrey, one of eight, said, "Papa, let's go out and touch the sun streaks." We got a picture for you and your dad, who was in the hospital from a car wreck. Audrey loved the picture and the sun rays, and her dad came home. I enjoy the country, taking pictures, old Harleys, and spending time with my grandchildren. This picture is very, very special. I am a retired union carpenter. I'll keep on clicking as long as my heart's ticking.

DEAMON, BECKY
I am a fourteen-year-old, home-schooled, ninth grade student. On my first photography class field trip, we went to our local park. "From Heaven To Hell" is a picture of a ford that goes across the Black River. On the day this picture was taken, the sun was very bright, and it was raining part of the time. Since the river was flooded, the water was flowing more rapidly than usual. This, contrasting with the bright, tranquil, more peaceful side of the river, gave the photo its name. This being the first photography contest I've ever entered, I never dreamed of actually getting results like this.

DEAN, GINA M.
Again, we're in the truck. Should I be happy this time or sad? Mia, Mommy, and Daddy are with me. I guess it won't be so bad! When we started this trip, I watched buildings, cars, and people everywhere. Now I see trees, birds, and look, Mommy . . . there are cows and horses over there! Daddy says we're going to Minnesota to build us a home with a big yard, a swingset, and some animals of our own! For now there's nothing left to look at, so off to dreamland I slip. Wake me when we've reached the end of another Dean family road trip!

DEFREITAS, MARCIA L.
This flower blooms only once a year and only at night. I thought a lot of people may never get to see such a bloom. I like to take unusual pictures for my own book. My camera goes everywhere with me. We live at Silver Dollar Golf and Trap Club, where I like to golf.

DEITZ, MARCELLA
I was so proud of my very first quilt, I had to take a picture of it. As I was about to snap the picture, to my surprise and delight, Chucky (a resident of the rock wall) quickly appeared between the rocks to have a look-see. He disappeared as quickly as he had appeared. It was truly a "snap" shot. I couldn't wait to share this photo with my quilting class. They got such a kick out of looking for Chucky. The contest ad was in the local paper that very week. The class encouraged me to enter my photo. What fun I've had with it.

DODSON, DIANA McMAKIN
"Sovereign Territory" was taken on a beautiful summer day on Mt. Evans in the Colorado Rockies. It was one of several photos taken of the mountain goat as I chased it through thigh-deep snow up the rocky slope, trying to get a picture of its face using my simple 35mm point-and-shoot camera (with clip-on telephoto lenses). An eighty-by-ten enlargement of "Sovereign Territory" hangs in my grandmother's home and is being published thanks to her passion for photography. Thank you, Grandmother. I love you.

DONOVAN, MAUREEN
Trying to capture this sunset took me four seasons of winters. To have the camera ready to view the scene as I could see it at just the right time was an ongoing trial and error. I'm very happy perseverance won out. My many attempts at photographing "A Winter Sunset" are just as memorable as the final photo.

DOUGHERTY, DONNA
While vacationing in Pennsylvania, I decided to take some pictures of the beautiful sunset. When I first got the pictures back and saw this one, I thought the camera had captured a vision of the Virgin Mary. That is the reason for the name. I was so shaken. Closer examination showed me it was actually a seagull. For me, though, each time I glance at this picture I will see a vision of the Virgin Mary.

DOUGHTY, CAROLINE
This photo is of my granddaughter, Brynn. She enjoys smelling and picking flowers in my garden. A picture like this makes my garden work enjoyable. I have been taking pictures for years, mostly of my children. Moments like this last forever.

DRAKULICH, MARCELLA
As these two grandchildren headed off for the first day of school on this beautiful August day, I couldn't resist taking this photo. This being Katie's first day of kindergarten and her having much anxiety, Matthew is reassuring her as they plod along into the unknown future. Thank you for selecting this photo; it made my day.

DROBENACK, MARGE
I am a photography major in college and plan on graduating this spring. Gram, Mom, and I took a day trip to New York City one Saturday. We were walking back from a photo supply store, and I noticed this homeless man sleeping on the sidewalk. I was actually very nervous about taking this picture, fearing the man would see me. This ended up being one of my favorite photos I've

ever taken. I feel I captured a moment that others might have overlooked.

DRUM, CINDY
The fawn was placed in my care by our local wild game commission. I have my veterinary assistant's degree and have volunteered for the commission for over twenty years. My cat, Whisper, fell in love with the fawn and did not leave its side for the three days it was in my care. The fawn was taken to a rehab center leaving a vacancy in Whisper's heart and home. She slept two nights where the fawn had spent time in my living room. My association with different animals each spring allows unique photo opportunities.

DUCH, JENNIFER M.
Did you ever turn around and see something so beautiful, so amazing, so inspiring that it left you breathless? Well, this was that moment for me. I never thought that the picture would do it justice. Boy, was I wrong. Photography has always been a small passion inside of me. I love capturing the moments and events that inspire and affect my life.

DURRIGAN, ANN B.
This picture was taken in Athol, MA, while visiting with friends. Sitting in their front living room, I heard this sudden thud like a brick hit the window. I ran outside to find this awesome bird totally stunned but clinging to a holder on the trunk of a tree. This enabled me to take a close up view and many pictures. I realized at the time that this was a rare opportunity, and I felt privileged and grateful. I'm originally from Ireland, and I've always enjoyed photography, especially of children and nature.

DUTCHER, BARBARA
My husband, Mike, his boss, Eric, and coworker, Tom, found the deer in a ditch full of water. It was near death. Mike brought it home and nursed it back to health. I took the picture when the dog, Coco, was baby-sitting in the backyard. Coco lost her sight a couple of years ago but treated the deer like her own child. When the deer, which we named Trego, could fend for himself, he was taken back to the Cranberry Marsh where he was found. To this day, he still visits once in a while.

DUVAL, MEREDITH
This picture was taken when my sister, mother, and I went sailing together for my sister's birthday. I took the picture so I could put it on my wall as motivation and as a reminder of my dream that someday my husband and I will be able to retire and sail off into the sunset together, like at the end of a romantic movie.

EATON, BETTY L.
Cousins Charles and Sidney enjoyed a great Thanksgiving with many family members. The picture was taken at the family ranch in Texas. The celebration continued with the pledge to the flag and everyone singing "America."

ECKEL, SHELLY
It was the summer of 2000. I received two orphaned raccoons to raise until they were old enough to return to the wilderness. They were

bottle-fed until they were able to eat solid foods. They loved to climb trees. This little guy is waiting behind a leaf until his brother gets close enough, and then he will jump out on him as they chase each other in the tree. After a few trips up the tree myself (usually at midnight) to cage them for their safety, I decided they were old enough to care for themselves. So I released them in a safe wooded area.

EDWARDS, KRISTEN
Photography is my passion and joy. My dream is to someday own my own photo studio. My family gave me a camera for my last birthday, and my photos have changed dramatically. Last Labor Day, we took our first camping trip in Colorado, having moved from Reno. This is a photograph of an area called Twin Lakes. The area's beauty touched my heart and soul. I hope you enjoy this picture as much as I enjoyed taking it.

EHRL, ADOLF J.
While on a weekend trip to New Hampshire, my family and I stopped to play a round of miniature golf. While playing, we came to this part of the course, which was set up as a mock moonshine operation. I had my brother-in-law pose among the kegs, with putter in hand. This photo got a lot of laughs in the family.

EINFINGER, WENDT
I like being creative and trying different things. Wanting to learn more about improving my photos, I had taken a course in photography. On the night I took this photo, I was driving with a friend and had taken a different route home, when I saw the old truck on a hill. I took a double take and about a minute later said, "Turn around; go back. I have to get a picture of that truck." I got out my camera and tripod and captured this photo. You just never know when an image will jump out at you.

ELKO, JOHN J.
Samba Nyak is a six-year-old Siberian husky who has a love for life and is truly my best, most devoted friend. Being in the U.S. Navy, Samba accompanied me overseas to Spain, where we lived for three years. Our house was only a few minutes walk from the ocean, where Samba loved to frolic in the sand and surf. Samba is a very friendly, intelligent, and playful husky who loves her master. As a final note, she is probably the most spoiled husky in the world, but she deserves it.

ELLIGAN, DONALD, JR.
I am a fairly serious amateur photographer. I've kept a camera in hand for a few years now. I love photography and the challenge of snapping a good and interesting photograph. This photo is of my daughter, Donese, taken as we left a function on a warm, bright, sunny day. Donese suddenly decided to try imitating fashion models that she had seen posing. Having my camera close by, I captured this shot. Shooting from the sun back into the shade of the building creates the dark background, which I thought was different in accentuating her colors. It's a nice memory for me.

ELLIS, MARY ANN
My photo of four ducks looking at one another

with a stream of sunlight reflecting between them was taken at the park in Buck County, Pennsylvania, with my first 35mm camera. After taking a photography class, I began experimenting with bracketing and utilizing different shutter speeds, using the manual features on my camera. I was surprised at the results. I have received numerous compliments and offers to purchase this photo primarily because of its contrast and simplicity. The photo was taken at sunset toward the end of the spring season approximately ten years ago with a Nikon N6006 camera, utilizing a 210mm zoom lens. I love taking pictures and have enjoyed this hobby for fifteen years. "For it is a photograph that expresses our emotions, provokes thoughts, and stimulates our imagination."

EMMING, JAN
It had been a nearly cloudless, torrid September in the Mojave Desert. I was surprised when just about at sunset a spectacular squall line of thunderstorms materialized from nowhere in under an hour. Sensing a dramatic opportunity, I raced the storms to the foothills of the Mualapac Mountains, where a magnificent stand of Joshua trees grows. Trying to balance artistry with safety, I made exposures ranging from one to fifteen minutes for the next several hours. The red cast on the Joshua tree is the result of my tail-lights as I waited in my car. I obtained many good photographs, but the lightning in this one is by far the best.

ESTERLINE, MIKE
We moved back to my hometown of Hillsdale, MI, to be with family after living in Florida for fifteen years. I travel past Sand Lake six days out of the week. I wanted to share with my family this beautiful sight. While showing my pictures at a family gathering, my grandmother told me how she and my great-grandmother would go there to admire the beautiful sight too. She reflected on the times they shared there, and now I will too . . . every time I look at this picture.

EVANS, PATTY J.
This is one of my animals, Thor. I'm always taking pictures. I have hundreds of photos I display. My kids and friends tease me over all my photos, plants, and pets. My pets are part of my family. My photos are precious to me. They're my memories of my children and grandchildren. One day I will pass on, and I'll leave behind my photos with the wonderful memories of them. To my daughter, Amy, and son, Allen, these pictures I take now will tell my life story from one generation to another. Our pictures live on forever. One hundred years from now, people will laugh, telling stories of pictures of the past.

FABIAN, HOLLY L.
I started taking photos to share our fun with other people on my website (www.geocities.com/dunvegan31). Friends then told me just how great they thought my photography was getting. I took this particular photo at the Detroit Zoo. I began to believe that maybe my pictures did show a piece of the world in a view no one else saw. Even though it was "Just A Frog" it looked so beautiful. I wanted to share it with everyone. Maybe it isn't really "Just A Frog" after all.

FAITH, EVE
We were living in southern Indiana during the summer of 1950 when I took this photo of my son, Ronnie. He was two-and-a-half years old and unaware that his photo was being taken. This photo will forever tug at my heart strings, bringing back precious memories of a moment in time so long ago. Ronnie had a long career in the U.S. Navy and retired as a chief petty officer. He kept his inquisitive nature throughout his life. We have resided in the Burlington and Durham areas of North Carolina for twenty-seven years.

FARINA, ANDREW DAVID
Despite trespassing across the farmer's field and getting buried up to my ankles in mud, I managed to get into position. The late day sun was fading fast, and the tree was showing off all its glory and contrast. Every once in a while, a scene captures our eye with a dramatic presence. Usually it appears when we least expect it, and I was just fortunate enough to have my camera.

FARRAR, ANDREW L.
I believe that a photo is worth a thousand words, and as an agriculture teacher in a rural community, I discovered that the newspaper editors use most photos sent to them for publication. Being asked to be the photographer for the centennial celebration for the church provided the opportunity to enhance my knowledge and skill.

FEEHERY, GERI
This photo was taken as I leaned far out of a window of Linderhof Castle in Germany. It was a truly remarkable view that I shared with my daughter, Jackie, who gave this trip to me as a gift. Freedom to take a picture in this beautiful country, considering our past history with Germany, is the reason for its name, "Freedom." I believe that someday the pictures I've enjoyed taking will be the visual vacations I'll take when I'm too old to travel.

FELICIANO, RACHAEL
I was amazed at how well this photo came out. Todd, my Pomeranian, was being tempted to trot at me as I lay on the floor with a treat between my lips. This is one of the things I enjoy doing with my dog. He is truly a musketeer with me while I take these types of pictures, though I think he likes the attention. This definitely will not be the last photo for this ". . . And One For All" dog.

FENDER, ETHEL M.
Since I live in the country, I'm always grabbing my camera and snapping animals and pets, hoping to capture on film a once-in-a-lifetime gem. A few years ago, my mom received from a friend this stuffed Paddington Bear for her birthday. Then last year for her birthday, from another friend, she received a kitten, which she named Lucky. Lucky soon learned that Patty's lap was just the right fit for him to snuggle in, so Lucky and Patty became "Bosom Buddies," seemingly for eternity. Lucky is fully grown now but still treasures Patty's lap.

FENDLEY, MISSY
This is a picture of my son, Kyle. We were taking pictures in the yard to mail for our Christmas

cards. He has always been very photogenic. He is also a good photographer. He is now eight years old and has a brother named Jackson.

FIELDS, HELEN M.
Thomas, one of my sons, is "Ready To Play." His mind and heart were thinking ball and not music. He was happy because he was on the way to the ball field. He took piano lessons until he was about thirteen years old. Then he begged to take guitar lessons. That was the end of piano playing. He did well with the guitar lessons. Now he is a man and watches someone else play ball, but he still plays his guitar and has taken lessons learning to play finger picking style guitar.

FINK, JILL
I specialize in photographing people and their most prized possessions . . . their pets! This particular cat was found abandoned outside a condominium complex. His owner took him in, treating the cat like a member of the family. Now that the cat is in a loving home and off the streets, his name has meaning for both pet and owner—Lucky.

FISHER, PHOTOGRAPHER
My daughter, who is three years old, loves butterflies, so I decided to plant a butterfly bush. When I looked out the window, I saw this beautiful butterfly, so I took this picture. I love to take pictures, and when I saw how well it turned out I wanted to send it in so everyone else could enjoy it as much as my daughter, Haley, and I have.

FLATHMANN, LISA
I took this photo in 1997 while scuba diving in Cayman Brac. The reason I call it "Paradise Below" is that it's beautiful and peaceful below the deep blue sea. I love taking photos, mostly of animals in their natural habitats. I took this photo with a Sealife Reefmaster underwater camera. I'm a dive master, and I teach snorkeling and skin diving.

FORBES, LOWELL P.
Spending time in the mountains means a great deal to me. The open spaces and the views of remote areas are worth the effort it takes to get there. This picture was taken on a trip to southwestern Colorado with some friends. The weather that day had been rainy up to this point. As I stood on top of this mountain, the clouds cleared for just a few minutes. This has always been one of my favorite photos. I never tire of the changing colors and variety in nature.

FORD, NORMA L.
Friends tease me about my very large purse, but I had my camera in it and was able to record the Bluebird Bus accident in West Virginia. The bus with fifty seniors aboard was on a narrow, twisty mountain road, when on a dangerous curve it got stuck. The driver ordered us off, then began to jockey the bus back and forth. But on one maneuver the bus shot right over the edge. We were very grateful to the driver for ordering us off the bus. However, this episode did not curtail our plans. We got another bus, and then water rafted to our next stop for lunch. We were a slightly shaken up, but hungry bunch of seniors.

FOSTER, EURA
"Early Morning On The Farm" was taken at sunrise on Thanksgiving 1998 when all my siblings, their children, and their grandchildren gathered to celebrate. Five siblings—Alvin M. Crews Jr., Charles G. Crews, Eura C. Foster, Winford Crews, and Etha C. Warren—all grew up on this farm where my paternal grandparents raised my dad, his five sisters, and his three brothers. The farm is now owned by Jimmy and Etha Warren. Because of the rich heritage this farm has provided, the lifelong dream of our parents has become a reality.

FOSTER, IRENE
Alaska is truly the last frontier. This photo was taken in Alaska at the Arctic Circle. Who would ever dream that a shot like this could be taken at 12:50 A.M.? As an amateur shutterbug, I try to have my camera ready for those once-in-a-lifetime shots.

FOSTER, KAREN
This is a picture of Popeye, my father's horse. When this picture was taken he was fifteen years old. He loves to go for a run after a long winter in his barn. Popeye is very happy when spring finally arrives.

FOULGER, BILLIE A.
I was born in Wyoming and have always loved the scenic Teton Mountain Range, and over the years I have taken many pictures there. In 2000, we traveled there once again to show this beautiful spot to our great-grandson, Nick. I was taking pictures of him, and when I looked up there was this scene. It was taken from the Signal Mt. campground, north of Jackson Hole, WY. I am seventy-two years old and just hope I can see those mountains many more times. I didn't realize that the large cloud looked like a bird's nest until I had the film developed.

FOVENYESSY, ATTILA
The proud Huli Wigmen of the Tari Basin, Papua New Guinea, still wear their traditional decorations and are famous for the decorated wigs that they wear. The Huli do not live in villages, but in scattered homesteads. They live in their immaculately and intensely cultivated valleys. This most remote region of the highland is beautiful and traditional. The woman and man often live in separate houses. Women are traditionally distrusted by men. The six-year-old Kila of Karita posed for my camera at 7:00 A.M. before I left her tribe.

FREDERIKSEN, JANET C.
This photo came about as a result of snapping pictures to use up my complete roll of film. While watching their dad fishing in the surf, my daughters entertained themselves by racing the waves up the beach. The expressions on their faces speak of sheer delight as I captured the emotion of the moment. They reminded me of silly sandpipers trying to escape the capture of the waves at their feet. This turned out to be the very last picture on my roll of film. It pays to be a shutterbug! The best photos are those not planned!

FRELING, KARI
This picture was taken as a birthday present for my mother. I wanted to give her something memorable, which would last forever, like the ongoing encouragement she has given me throughout my life. While playing around with filters, I took this picture of her favorite flowers. When she saw it she was proud, but what I don't get to tell her is how proud I am of her. She has worked so hard to get me where I am today, and this picture was just a token of my affection and admiration for a very special person.

FRENCH, ALLISON
For my eleven-month-old son, Garrett, nothing stops him from going for walks with his grandpa. Garrett had only been walking for one week before I took this picture. This photograph was taken at my parents' vacation home in the Adirondack Mountains in Stratford, NY. This is a place the family goes to enjoy the outdoors and just spend time together. From taking walks to sitting by the campfire our most precious memories are from here. This picture captures the love and companionship that Garrett shares with his grandpa.

FRIED, GRACE JEAN
I'd always wanted to visit Iceland, and when I finally did, I believe the "little people" welcomed me with many images. The magic of nature provided unexpected visions, but "Trolls' Work" was the most amazing.

FRIES, AMY
This photo is of one of the Bernoulli Fountains in Rome, Italy. I took this snapshot while my family and I were vacationing there. I never thought it would come out so well. Now, I am seeing pictures in everything and anything. I consider photography to be a wonderful medium, and I love watching with the light.

FRIESEN, ELISHA
It's said that if you don't stop and look around, you might miss something wonderful. I have captured only one of many wonderful things out there. No matter where you are, just look up at the world and see the beauty around you. It will only happen once, and then it's gone. You don't have to go to the Grand Canyon to get a good picture. All you have to do is to look in your own backyard, and you can capture a moment in time that will last forever.

FROST, CARLA S.
From the ice, which once consumed her, she'll emerge, her mighty mast and sail, carved by the breath of angels, ready for one last voyage to the sun.

GABRIEL, RICK
My wife, Dee Dee, and I have traveled many places by car. We have taken so many memorable photos, but we just don't have time to get them all developed. This picture was one of the lucky ones. I wonder, in sixteen years how many more wonderful shots we have missed. We were just driving by this one.

GALLE, JOHN L., SR.
I was the assistant chief of the Windom, MN, vol-

unteer fire department. I retired in 1982 after twenty-nine years of service. After retirement, the chief asked me if I would come out and take some photos of a building burn drill. We would be looking for good and bad procedures. We let the building burn to the ground when the drill was completed. After the drill, I found some exposures left in my camera and noticed the chief walking between me and the fire. I asked him to hold it right there, composed my picture, and here is the end result.

GALLIGAN, CAROL
As an artist, my focus has been on the last five years I experienced with my mother, who recently died of Alzheimer's disease. I was consumed with photographing her and came to realize these photos had to be part of my final mother/daughter installation. I do not consider myself a photographer and worried about the quality of the photos. However, the negatives I accumulated over the years had to be developed, and it had to be done by me regardless of the results. This photo doesn't come close to showing the beauty and strength of this woman.

GEORGE, ROBBIE
This is a photo that captures a rare moment in time. The lightning and rainbow together show how fickle Mother Nature can be. She can be bright, beautiful, and warm, yet on the other hand, she can be dark, scary, and cold.

GILLEN, REBECCA
The ducks were a pretty fun bunch of guys to shoot. I just showed up to the park, and they wanted to play. We all had a good day that day.

GILLENWATER, PAULA
This is a photo of our favorite cat that likes to sleep in clay pots all over our yard. You can find her in some strange places sleeping peacefully. My family loves cats, and we love to take pictures of animals.

GLASGOW, MARCELLA A.
My photo was taken during a family vacation trip visiting my brother in Ocala, FL. He has a very lovely home with a large water fountain, in the photo (transported on a crane), operating in the front lawn area. The picture was posed with my brother's Great Dane, Dior, and his award winning miniature horse, Magic Man. It took quite a few shots and loads of patience, plus the right time of day, to produce the wanted results. I love taking photos that turn out unique, using a lovely background with an animal/pet foreground.

GLIWA, CARRIE
I took this photo while I was vacationing at my aunt's house in New Jersey. The dog's name is Blue, and he loves to swim in the pool.

GODBOUT, LOUISE
Photography has been a hobby of mine since I was old enough to buy film on my own. Over the years, one of my best friends kept encouraging me to participate in a photography contest. This photograph was taken next to our house during a storm. That's my favorite time to go out there. Entering this contest has a special meaning

because my friend has since passed away. This is for you, Jojo!

GORDON, ELAINE
This is a picture of my son, David, a junior at Winslow High School in Winslow, ME. He is a halfback on our varsity soccer team and enjoys sports very much. David plans to go on to college to study computer science next year.

GOSNELL, KAYE
This picture was taken in the fall of 2000 in Gatlinburg, TN. I enjoy taking pictures of God's creations. There's no limit to what He can do. I like taking pictures of my grandson, Drew, and creating scrapbooks of him. I have scrapbooks of my own sons, Travis and Trent.

GRAHAM, CARLA
This is a picture of my daughter, Evyn, in front of her Christmas tree. Each year, we have at least five trees in our home. Evyn's tree is a small tree with small ornaments. She loves to go in her room and look at the lights at night. I took this photo because it shows the happiness of a child at Christmas.

GRANATA, HEATHER
As a college student majoring in wildlife and fishery biology and management, I have long had a passion for nature and animals. Although my primary focus will include mammals, my love for birds will never cease. This photograph is of our sun conure, just one of my family's many parrots. The title of this photo was derived from his name. I chose to take this picture to capture the elegance, beauty, and personality found in such creatures. Without Carl and Linda Moss, I would not have known the love and companionship that these birds so freely give.

GREER, JASON
I am a twenty-six-year-old amateur photographer and college student. My favorite subject matter is landscape photography. The grandeur of urban and natural environments fascinates me. I am interested in any opportunity for my photographs to be recognized. I am also eager to capture many more unique and delightful scenes on film.

GRONEMEYER, SUSAN
Stripe wormed her way into my heart by waiting faithfully for me at the back door every morning. Even though I thought it was love, she was more interested in food, and lots of it. Now, she is an actively participating member of the household, which includes "guarding" the Christmas tree.

GROVER, ERIN E.
This photo is of the St. Louis Cathedral in New Orleans, LA. I took this photo on a whim while in New Orleans on a university trip. I wanted to capture New Orleans at its finest. This picture was taken mid-morning with a disposable camera. I was surprised at how well the picture turned out. I live in Pittsburgh with my parents and my brother, Daniel. I graduated from Edinboro University of Pennsylvania, where I majored in education.

GUAY, EVIE MAY
I have loved nature from my earliest childhood

days. Being outdoors uplifts me and fills me with gratitude. It delights me being able to capture scenes that vary with light, weather, and the changing seasons. I especially love to capture those special moments in the lives of family and friends. This scene is of Burr Pond near Winsted, CT, where our family has enjoyed many days of swimming, fishing, and picnicking. Here I was fascinated by lovely fall colors and the exposed rocks, which in spring and summer are covered by water.

HAHN, LORRAINE
Sammy is a terrific samoyed who lives next door to me. One hot day, he came from the groomer looking twenty pounds lighter and came to my door to show me his new do. I grabbed a throw-away camera and told him to smile! Now, I'm not a picture-taker. They never come out the way that I envision them. Usually everyone's head is missing from the shot! Well, this is the result, and I'm delighted that you chose to publish his picture. It is a great tribute to a loyal and wonderful pet.

HALL, ANGELIA
I've never really thought of myself as a cat-lover. I started out with one, and now I have seven. Some I bought, and some were given to me. Out of all seven, these two truly seem to be best friends, and after a hard morning's work of bird-watching, it seems as if they are daydreaming of cardinal soup and blackbird pie, completed with a smile. I guess I can say now that I'm truly a cat-lover, and I love each and every one for them for their very different personalities and the joy and peace they give me.

HAMES, WILLIAM
This image is of a house in Hammerfest, Norway. I was traveling by ship on a Norwegian coastal voyage when we called on the port of Hammerfest. Passengers were given two hours of shore leave to explore the town. I had wandered through the city center and had just finished shooting film in an old cemetery. I was walking back towards the ship when I saw this house. I knew it had the potential for a grand photograph. Thanks for the opportunity to share the image I captured.

HAMRICK, RANDY
Fall is a time of cool weather and beautiful colors. This photograph warms my heart. The bright, vivid colors remind me how wonderful fall can be if you just slow down and look around. I've always enjoyed capturing moments in time on film to look back on. Some photos make you frown and some make you smile, but they all stir your emotions and make you feel something. I hope this photograph makes everyone grin with pleasant thoughts of fall and beautiful colors!

HANNA, GARY
This photograph was taken in Kruger Park in South Africa. I was in South Africa with a group of photographers with the People to People Ambassador Program. I enjoy sharing travel photographs.

HARGREAVES, FRANCES BRIGID
I love taking pictures of sunsets. I am in awe of the many colors, variations, and patterns in the

sky when the sun disappears on the horizon. To me, my camera is an extension of my imagination. Cloud formations and architecture are also interesting to me because of the angles and the depth of shadows in the different atmospheres. It's always fun taking pictures just to see the results, so I always have my camera with me. My nationality is Irish. My husband of forty years is English. Our two children, Sean and Rebecca, are very talented. Sean is a production designer in movies, and Rebecca is a fashion designer in New York. We love them dearly. I am retired.

HARLACKER, JOHN A.
Advertising is for everybody, including my pet dog, Shep. Why would anyone write about their pet dog, Shep, advertising? Think about it. Your pet dog barks, and he's advertising that someone is on your property. Your dog growls, and he's advertising his dislike for something. His ears go up, and he's advertising that something is close by. He wags his tail for you, and he's advertising his love for you and letting you know everything is fine in your household. So a dog that advertises shows his love for the family. So wag your tail and learn from your pet dog how to show your love.

HARMON, SANDRA
It was a privilege to be able to capture this view. Mother Nature has taken care of herself and all that belongs within her spectrum by providing for the seclusion and reverence of her inner peace, a beautiful gift.

HARPEL, PENNIE
This cabin is along one of my favorite day hikes, Marion Mine in Rye, CO. As my dog, Rainey, and I hiked in, I was overwhelmed by the beauty of the untouched snow cascading across this peaceful place. It was a majestic, breathtaking view unlike any other time of the year.

HARRIS, ANTHONY
This is a picture of my son, Tavares, at one year old on our family vacation in Florida, and, as you can see, he's having the time of his life. Since the age of six months, Tavares has always been such a character. Whenever I go for the camera it seems he just knows what to do in front of it. I think if I had purposefully tried to arrange this photo, I would've tried a hundred times and wouldn't have succeeded. Isn't it always that way though? When you least expect it, you end up being blessed with a priceless moment in time that somehow justifies life and all the beautiful things in it.

HASELBAUER, MARLENE
This is a photograph of my first granddaughter, Kristina Elena, and my loving dog, Regalo ("gift"), on the morning of Thanksgiving Day. I sent out this photo with my Christmas cards that year. I do not take photographs well at all, and I was amazed to see how beautiful both their expressions are captured. I only wish that I could be that lucky again and do something similar with my second granddaughter, Karesa Maria, and her dogs, Lady and Cricket. I will treasure this forever.

HAWRYLO, FRANK
This is a photo of two of my grandchildren. Stephie is holding her younger brother, Jacob, in a peek-a-boo photo, taken through the branches of a blue spruce on our front lawn. The photo captures the various shadings of the pine needles and surrounding area, with an opening in the branches providing a unique frame, highlighting two precious faces. I am a proud grandfather, who took this photo at the spur of the moment in mid-afternoon and was surprised and very pleased with Mother Nature's contribution to the beauty of this picture. It's a moment of play preserved forever.

HEAD, WALTER L.
I am a marine currently serving twenty-four years of service on active duty in the United States Armed Forces. My family and I are from Griffin, GA, and we are stationed in Camp Lejeune, NC. We were on a family outing in the park when I captured the special true moment of nature in action. Three white seagulls decided to join a duck in a moment of peace in the picture "What's Up, Duck!" It reflects on our lives as humans, which brings to mind the way we should join together in love and peace in this world regardless of race, religion, or sex.

HEDDEN, ADELIA
When I saw this field and old windmill, it looked so peaceful and pretty. I just had to take the picture. That's what I look for when driving around the country. Taking pictures is something I really enjoy doing.

HEFNER, REBECCA
I am an avid gardener. I work in my flower gardens all spring and summer. This is my grandson, Josh, in the picture. When Josh visits he takes every step I take. He loves flowers as much as I do. Like me, he can tell you the names of all my daylilies and irises. The bond between grandmother and grandson has been made stronger through our love of flowers. We all should take the time to enjoy the smell of flowers, as Josh does.

HEITZMAN, JOSEPHINE
Taken at tulip time in the Skagit Valley of Washington, this photo won a blue ribbon at "Art in the Pickle Barn" during the Tulip Festival. It is named "Harmony" for the sense of peace one receives when out in the tulip fields.

HEMPEL, ALEXANDRA A.
Take a moment to think about history. Think about how much more vivid and real some of it is because of what we can see on film. In this picture, I've captured a piece of history in progress. You can see old County Stadium almost handing over the torch as Miller Park is being constructed right next to it. I shot this more than one year after the tragic crane collapse. At the very bottom, you can see flowers still woven in the temporary fence, left in memory of three lives lost. One picture with so much meaning. . . .

HENNION, DARRELL
This is a photo of my wife, Betty. She has put makeup on to look like a rock star. It was Halloween, and she was going trick-or-treating

with our son, Cody. She got a lot of comments on how great she looked.

HENRY, SUSZETTE
I've always been an animal-lover and have always been taking care of them, small and large. The kitten in the box has been adopted by a loving family. I'm very strict about who adopts my spoiled animals. My family, my friends, and even strangers bring me abandoned or injured animals. Someday, I want to buy a ranch for my expanding "family." I feel we have to be their voices since they, along with children, can't speak for themselves. We have to be the ones to speak out for them against abuse.

HENSLEY, RUSTY
This is a photo of my three-year-old son, Jamie, doing what he loves most—playing outside in the dirt. I took this picture during the summer of 2000 in the backyard of our home. I was enchanted by the intense look on Jamie's face as he sat on the ground with his little dump truck and shovel, being so careful not to spill any of the dirt as he loaded up his truck. As his mother, this photo represents one of those cherished moments in time that I wanted to capture and keep forever.

HERBERT, BONNIE
I love taking photographs, so when my family went to Europe for two weeks I was in Heaven with my camera. I took a lot of beautiful pictures on our trip, but this is one that I particularly liked. The architecture was so beautiful, and the ruins were so huge and majestic that I wanted to capture them forever.

HERK, SANDRA L.
This is my grandson, Josh. I care for him and his baby brother, Hayden, almost every day. On any non-rainy day, we will walk through the flower gardens, and Josh will have to stop and smell every flower on the way. This picture, showing a little boy's sweet nature and gentle side, melts my heart. I've always enjoyed taking pictures, but adding five new grandchildren to one older grandson in less than two years has brought about a whole new dimension in picture-taking for me.

HERNANDEZ, CHRIS A.
While traveling from southwestern Nebraska with my granddaughter, Big L. (Papa has affectionately called her that since birth), we crested a hill, and on the other side we happened upon a seemingly timeless moment. Two longhorn steers appeared to be frozen in time in front of the ol' homestead. Fortunately, with camera in tow, the light was right, the subject was special, and the memory was captured; everything just seemed to "click." One might try to describe a scene such as this, but a picture is worth a thousand words.

HERRON, WILLIAM L.
Though my master refers to me as Purrfect Cat, the name registered with my veterinarian is Xie-Xie (pronounced "Shay-Shay"). This Chinese name, written in Pinyin—the romanticization of Chinese characters as developed in the People's Republic of China—translates as "thank you." Now isn't that a ridiculous name for a cat! Some folks describe my coloring as orange tabby, while

others label me butterscotch; in England a cat with my color and markings is identified as marmalade. In this regard, my master affectionately calls me Little Miss Marmalade. So you see, I'm no ordinary alley cat!

HILL, EDNA

This photograph was taken on December 23, 1991, in the driveway of my sister and brother-in-law's home in Louisville, KY. This date happened to be their fortieth wedding anniversary. A light snow had fallen during the night. As I went for the morning newspaper, I saw the tire tracks. The design was so unique, I grabbed the camera and snapped.

HILLAGE, PAM

This picture was taken on my first camping trip ever. Waking up at the crack of dawn every day wasn't making for a fun vacation until I noticed how to enjoy the peace and quiet before the day began. It was a very memorable summer vacation.

HILLIARD, CINDIE

My name is Cindie Hilliard. I live in Fairview, UT, with my husband, Casey, and three children: Cody, Joey, and Shaelie. Some of my hobbies are puzzling, cleaning my house, and playing with my dog, Buddy. I've spent a lot of time dressing him up and taking photos of him. He's part pug and part Chihuahua. I've taken many different photos of sunsets from my back door. I've had a lot of compliments on this "Firestorm" photo from family and friends, so I decided to send it in.

HINTZE, ROSEMARIE

Samantha, my tenth grandchild came for a visit since her mother had to leave. So to keep her busy, I let her sit in my bay window looking at all the decorated homes. When nightfall came, the houses started to light up. She got all excited! All of a sudden she turned, sat down, lifted her little hand, and said, "Where's Ho Ho (her word for Santa Claus)?"

HOGAN, DEBBIE

We adopted Rascal in September of 1994, after much prompting from our children when we decided on a cat for a pet. So Rascal entered our lives. He was one year old and absolutely adorable and ready to be a part of our family. His wanting to be a family member is evident in this picture. This particular day, to our immense amusement, he decided he wanted to share my youngest daughter, Amanda's, sandwich. So he climbed up in her lap, promptly inquired, "Can I have a bite?", and helped himself.

HOHN, JULIE

The Jasper fire started in the Black Hills in August of 2000. I took this picture from our house at the end of August. It was about twelve miles from us when it was contained. This particular fire cloud started numerous smaller fires from the lightning inside it. The Black Hills fire took approximately ninety thousand acres.

HOLCOMB, ARLENE M.

This photo is of my granddaughter, Ashley, and a baby sparrow that had just fallen out of its nest. I put the bird in a planter, and Ashley and the little

bird became totally mesmerized with each other. I ran for my camera, and since they were in the shade, I also grabbed my gold reflector. My son held the reflector, so I did not need to disturb the moment with a flash. I managed to take a couple of photos before either of them moved. Ashley kept whispering, "Hi, Baby Bird," so that is what I named the photo.

HOLLINGWORTH, FLORENCE

A rainstorm in the desert is a precious gift. In this valley, the storms usually skirt around us, as they had been all afternoon. At about five o'clock, I happened to see the beauty of the sky from my own doorstep. For the gift of "seeing with the eyes of my heart," I am grateful. My camera is a close friend and a great teacher. Nature is truly the art of God.

HOOKS, CYNTHIA

I love cats. I love everything about cats. While at the zoo, I always make it a point to visit the lions and tigers. As I stood waiting to see a tiger, this one walked out past the trees, stopped, and looked at me as if to say, "Here I am. Take my picture." So I did. I love this picture.

HORNSBY, SHERRY

We love to eat our suppers together. Mego is loved by his family—his mother, Sherry, his sisters, Miranda and Melissa, and his dog brother, Doctor Kujo. Kujo cleans Mego's ears out and his only eye. A pitbull got his other eye. I wouldn't trust a pitbull around anyone. Mego and Kujo take care of each other in different ways. As you can tell, Mego is one of our family. Mego is one of the sweetest you'd ever want. Mego also loves his grandparents, Leona and Richard, his aunt, Pam, and Halls cough drops.

HOSTING, CAROL

There are so many things this picture calls to mind about that day that I couldn't possibly tell it all. This poem gives a good idea how the day went. "That was the day the motor wouldn't start; / That was the day we saw pelicans scoop fish from the water; / That was the day we caught no fish; / That was the day we suffered from sunburn; / That was the day I wondered why we go through so much to have fun; / That was the day this sunset made me reflect; / It was worth it."

HOTZ, CARMELINDA

I just love to take pictures wherever I go, whether it's at a home party or on my travels. Argentina is a beautiful country, and I did enjoy seeing all the interesting places, especially the ranches and horses. I love to travel, and wherever I go I take my camera.

HOWARD, DIANE

This is a photo of a great-horned sheep that I took on a mother and son trip to the South Dakota Black Hills during the fall of 1997. I've been taking photos since my early teens, mostly while on vacations with my folks. The tradition and love for photography still exist today. My dream is to someday take photos of nature and wildlife all around the world.

HOWELL, MARTHA G.

Every year in the fall we travel to the mountains of Virginia to pick apples. This tranquil scene was captured on the road to the orchard. My special interests are in nature and scenic photography. I am very appreciative of my family's patience when asked to stop the car, in sometimes awkward places, to photograph a wildflower, rock formation, or cool mountain stream.

HOWLAND, JENNIFER

Lindsay is four-and-a-half months old in this picture and is dressed as a pea pod for her first Halloween. She is sitting in a 1750s children's Carver chair that was originally purchased by her great-grandparents. She is the third generation of our family to use this chair. This photo brings a smile and a chuckle to everyone who sees it. Within moments of this being taken, she became very preoccupied with chewing and squeezing the stuffed pea perched under her chin!

HUNT, JULIE

Fancy belongs to my boyfriend's mom. She loves to go outside and roll around in the dirt and grass. They got her from a friend who found her as a stray. I really got into pictures when I started doing creative memories and scrapbooks. Now I take pictures of just about everything. I saw Fancy playing in the grass, and I thought it would make a great picture for my scrapbook.

HUSSELMAN, BRUCE L.

"August Moon" was taken at our weekend summer home at Raccoon Lake, fifty miles west of Indianapolis, IN. I went out on the patio to fold up some chairs and saw the moon peeking through the trees and reflecting on the water. I have always been so grateful to God for the beautiful sunsets, and when I saw this view I just had to get a picture of another of God's beautiful gifts.

IRONFIELD, SCOTT

Among other interests I have, I am a G.I. Joe collector, not for future profit, but because I still have most of the imagination I had as a kid. I enjoy amusing myself, friends, and family with scenes I set up in my game room or outside. This picture (one of the many different scenes) is actually the third and final shot of a series. The first has just the one Joe sitting on the rock reading the map. The second shot has the bad guy sneaking up on Joe with knife raised. Enter the second Joe for the last shot. Don't even think about it.

JACKSON, DARLA

I think the title of this picture speaks for itself. These are my one-year-old twin sons, Daniel and David. We told them we were going outside to go swimming. I guess we weren't fast enough because they headed out the dog door. I just happened to have the camera to take pictures of them swimming, but this turned out to be the best picture of all!

JACKSON, J. J.

My camera is my "great escape." On December 5, 1990, my brother, Bud, was brutally murdered and robbed. April 19, 1995, I was late for an appointment at the Oklahoma City Murrah Building. At 9:02 A.M. the world saw the rubble and aftermath of calculated evil. I assisted the medical examiners office with death notifications. April 1996, I accompanied bombing survivors to D.C. We lobbied for the anti-terrorism bill, and it passed. I moved to Jackson Hole, WY, to escape the bombing site. "Shadows And Snow" is a beautiful day while hiding behind my friend, my camera.

JACOBS, CHRISTY
While watching a Challenger League baseball game, Kelsie would not stop barking. Every time the ball was thrown, hit, or pitched, she would bark and yelp. Finally, I realized that she wanted to go out and play ball with the kids. There wasn't anything I could do to make her stop barking, and she was starting to make a scene. About that time, a parent of one of the players came up and gave Kelsie a baseball that her son had in his bag and said, "In the Challenger League, everyone gets a chance to play!"

JAMES, KAREN
For someone whose tendency it is to break her camera rather than capture breathtaking moments, I am certainly having Ansel Adams delusions of grandeur. It had rained every day that we were on Bora-Bora, but as the skies were clearing one afternoon, I was able to photograph this magnificence. The camera, however, did not manage to detect the pose of poodle-sized, dive-bombing mosquitoes that were also happy for sunlight and fresh meat, which launched me flailing down the beach! I'd like to thank my mom and dad for making everything possible.

JANKAVICH, RITA
I spent a cold winter day making "Henry" from an old bed sheet and dressing him in our twin boys' clothes. Then my husband and I wanted to surprise them with our guest. We decided to place "Henry" in the bathroom where the boys would always race each other to get in first. We still laugh today when we look at that picture, a tell of those first moments of surprise.

JANSEN, LINDA S.
On October 16, my oldest son, James, and his future wife, Kristen, bussed from Washington State to Michigan to be married on my birthday (October 19). I had made all the arrangements and paid all fees in waiting for this special occasion and birthday present to take place. The weather was questionable for those three days they traveled, but on that special fall day, it became extra special as the weather turned out to be beautiful! To mark that very special day of my birthday and the marriage of my eldest son, we the wedding party (James, Kristen, Uncle Chuck, and I), decided a picture should be taken where history still stands and more history was made, in this still working courthouse.

JEDELE, ROBIN
This photo is dedicated to the memory of my father, Robert Jedele. It was taken on the seven-mile beach during the Jedele family reunion.

JENKINS, TIMOTHY ALLEN
A Cherokee American Indian, this artist also enjoys clay sculpting and training his boxers,

Smooch and Una Ageya. He inherited his love for photography from his father who spent years as a professional photographer. He is completely devoted to his family and loves being a brother, uncle, youth pastor, and a husband. He's grateful for his mother who taught him life's values. He gave his heart to God in 1987, and he works and lives to serve the one who died for him. He took this photo while celebrating his fifth anniversary with his high school sweetheart, Becky, who collects lighthouses.

JOHNSON, ASHLEY
This photo was taken on a very special and memorable trip to London, England. I come from a family of camera buffs, so I love to capture the beauty of foreign places when I travel. That is why this picture is so important and unique to me! I took this picture because Big Ben looked so spirited and dignified that warm April afternoon. I always take my camera with me when I travel with my family, because you never know what captivating and exquisite historic sight you might see along the way.

JOHNSON, DERRICK
This is my youngest son, Erik. We had just watered the backyard and let the kids out on the patio to play. As you can see, little Erik went a little further, to the part of the yard that had no grass.

JOHNSON, JUDY
The better part of my summers have been spent on our boat with my husband, Bill, and sons, Bill and Erik. I have never taken photography classes; I just happened to be in the right place at the right time. I've always enjoyed the peace and beauty of the sunset on the Great South Bay.

JONES, HUNTER
Precious memories are recaptured through photographs. A great photograph is absolutely priceless because it will live forever and offer a single moment to reflect on in the past. This photo of my rottweiler, Santos, displays a wide smile personifying his cuteness and mischievousness. During his first experience with snow, Santos gobbled it up as a gourmet delight. I caught this priceless moment while taking photographs of Santos for my 1999 Christmas cards. I will cherish this shot forever and savor my two-year adventure in Germany with him.

JONES, PETER E.
I am retired from the U.S. Coast Guard, so my photographic interests have always had a nautical theme, with lighthouses as my favorite subject. I have taken many color photographs of this light, but this photograph is one of my first attempts at Nauset Light in black-and-white.

KANNES, ALFREDINA
My mother, Matilda Candreva, came from a farm in San Giacomo, Cosenza, Italy, in the '50s. She loved to grow her own vegetables. At Pinewood Hall, a senior citizens' complex located in Roselle, NJ, she built high wooden boxes, filled them with soil in the back of the building, and allowed residents with green thumbs to enjoy gardening in warm weather. We especially enjoyed that Mom shared her tomato bounty with family

and friends. Although Mom passed away this October at the age of ninety-one, I'll always treasure her love of growing her own tomatoes.

KAYLOR, EVELYN
On a recent trip to Plimoth Plantation Village in Plymouth, MA, I shot this picture of one of the chickens there. Normally, I would not consider a picture of a chicken interesting, but this one had very beautiful coloring. I was pleased to catch the chicken as she took a step, which added a realistic tone.

KAYLOR, VONNIE
My husband, Fred, and I love dogs. Riley belongs to my son, Allan, and his wife, Kristen. I am an avid scrapbooker and love to take photos and make memory albums. We were at a family gathering eating and celebrating outdoors, when my other son, Scott, and his wife, Jill, noted that Riley got a paper plate for some goodies also.

KELLER, COLLEEN J.
The picture means a lot to me. My father had A.L.S., Cal Gerhit's disease, and we took him to see his sister, Dorothy. The Grand Canyon is a very beautiful place, in which one can lose himself spiritually. When I think of Arizona, I will always remember my papa's smile during the entire trip. This picture captures the beauty of the canyon.

KENNEDY, FRAN
In March 2000, my friend Karen Sinesky told me one of her dreams was to own a Yorkie and name her Lucy. After numerous phone calls to breeders and answering newspaper ads, we visited a local breeder who had six precious puppies. I remember Karen holding Lucy and looking her in the eyes, asking, "Do you want to be my Lucy?" Six weeks later, Lucy became Ms. Lucy of McFarland, and our lives have been intertwined ever since. I was praying to God to send me something to brighten my life and give me joy. Thank you, God, for Lucy!

KIDDER, LARK
This is a picture of my little sister, Tricia. It was taken one afternoon last autumn while we were playing outside on the front lawn. My sister is one of my favorite subjects because she projects the innocence and beauty of childhood by not being afraid of either the camera or posing in front of it. I felt this shot was very unique because of its direct composition in relation to the light source. The glimmer of my sister's eyes perfectly captures the honest and tender nature of her personality.

KIMMEL, LESTER
This is a photo of one of the squirrels that comes into our backyard to eat off the ears of corn that I place there on a post for them. I took this picture because I really enjoy watching the squirrels come and eat the corn. I caught this one squirrel in a unique way of eating.

KLASSEN, STEPHANIE
This is a photograph of my grandpa's farm in Nebraska. It was a beautiful winter day, and I wanted to capture it on film. The building in the picture is the chicken house where my cousins

and I spent many summers playing with the baby chicks. I could tell a hundred stories about our crazy adventures on the farm. I really enjoy photography and teach second grade in Cathedral City.

KNIGHT, INGRID E.
My eight-month-old granddaughter, Jessica, was visiting us in Colorado from Texas in early December. After a day of the hustle and bustle of the Christmas season, we came home and put her in the high-chair to fix her food. She was so exhausted from the outing, she fell asleep, her head hanging down. So we put the Christmas pillow under her head for comfort. Jessica and her sister, Holly, my only grandchildren, are my favorite photo subjects. I also like to hike and snowshoe the Rocky Mountains, and I never leave home without my camera.

KNIGHT, TYLER
I am twelve years old. I took this picture on a weekend trip to San Diego with my family. I asked my mom to use her camera, so I could take a picture of a blue jay playing in the bushes nearby. I would like to take photography classes in the future.

KNOLL, RUTH
My husband and I were involved in everything regarding Elvis; we had shows twice yearly. We got Elvis' band and backup group, J. D. Sumpter and the Stamps, here. At this show they were singing "How Great Thou Art." My daughter, being special, was so taken with them and there music.

KNUDSEN, CARL E.
I call my cat Puddin' because of the splotches of butterscotch coloration on her face and body. She is truly wonderful, and it has been easy for us to spoil each other with our affection. We are alone together much of the time, but being alone with her is not being lonely. Puddin' is as sweet as her name implies, and she would still be sweet by any other name.

KNUTH, SHEILA
After completing my first photography class, I decided to venture out and test my skills. I love nature, especially wildlife, but when I discovered this photo opportunity, I realized that whether it be a majestic bull elk or a tree that has surrendered to the elements, it is all breathtakingly beautiful. My love for photography began with this photo, taken in Estes Park, Colorado, in 2000.

KOSTER, EUGENE J.
I always enjoyed picture-taking, even as a young boy with my box camera. This photo was taken as I cruised the Hudson River with my family and friends on the yacht, *Star of America*. The happy occasion was the wedding celebration of my niece, Dianne Searfoss, and Michael Morin. I happened to be up on deck as we passed the flowers and saw the building bathed in the glistening sunlight. I seized the moment and took this photo. I've taken many pictures but never entered a contest until this one, and I feel deeply honored for the recognition.

KOWALCHICK, ANDREW JOSHEPH
This picture was taken on Chincoteague Island, Virginia, as an afternoon storm came in between the bay and the ocean. Living in Maryland, on Kent Island, our family enjoys the water. Nature pictures on the Chesapeake Bay and the ocean are unlimited, and it almost always seems that for some reason only very few make it into a frame.

KOWALESKI, JOSEPHINE
This is a photo of my mother, Belle Sheets, reading to her great-grandchildren. She was always reading to them for their or just her own pleasure. She was also always writing poetry. She has been gone now for four years, and we will miss her. But all our pictures are great memories. I was always taking them, mostly of all our family and friends.

KRATKA, ANNETTE
I found Buster a little over five years ago along the side of the road. He had been hit and was in pretty bad shape, but he had the most wonderful eyes that said, "Help me." Being the animal-lover that I am, I scooped him up and took him to the vet. Seven days and fifty-two stitches later, he was mine. He came into a home that had been cats-only for many years, and he immediately ingratiated himself to the point where if the cat had the couch, he got the chair.

KRITOS, MARIA
This photo was taken during my honeymoon stay on the breathtakingly beautiful island of Santorini. Apart from its picturesque whitewashed houses built on cliffs and its crystal blue Aegean waters, Santorini also has friendly stray cats which add to the island's character. The mom cat and its baby kitten featured in this photo befriended my husband and I one morning when I hand-fed them some bread. Instantaneously, throughout our remaining stay, the charming duo kept us company on our terrace—which is where they are caught napping comfortably on film.

KRUEGER, DARLENE
This picture represents one of the best characteristics of my dog, Spud—his magnificence. He is the best friend that I could ever have. He is always with me. When I'm happy he shares my joy, when I am sad he comforts my heart, and when I'm angry and my judgement is clouded, his presence and love offer me a clear path.

KUKLA, JODI
This is a photo of my husband, Aaron, preparing for a relaxing night of fishing. It was taken on a beautiful March evening on our vacation to Gulf Shores, AL. This picture is special to us, not only because of its scenic beauty, but also because it portrays Aaron's passion for fishing.

LABELLA, DEBBIE
Photography has been a passion for me all my life. I love horses and wildlife and capturing those special moments of nature with photographs. I took a trip to Lexington, KY, to tour the countryside and see the city. During that month, artists had created a display of the horses of Lexington. Hand-painted statues were scattered throughout the city; they were fascinating to see. I took many

photos, but this one I thought was special and worth sharing with others.

LADD, SHIRLENE
This is a picture of my grandson, Adam. He and his sister love to see the wind blowing the flag and try to touch it. Adam knows the "Pledge of Allegiance" and what the flag stands for. We are very proud of him. I take pictures all the time, and I'm proud of this one.

LAKIN, DAVID W.
This is a photo I took while visiting my parents in Athens, GA. It was a beautiful, warm day in August, and there was a group of butterflies lingering in the front yard. I don't take pictures as often as my wife, but when I saw this beauty of nature, I had to savor it! Then she secretly entered the picture into a contest, and here it is!

LANSBERRY, TERI
This is a photo of our cat, Jasper, or Mr. Man as he likes to be called. It wasn't long after being brought home from the shelter that he acquired his "catitude." My husband, Ken, and I have two other cats, Charmaine and Chloe, and one dog, Pepper. We own and operate a pet-sitting service in Santa Rosa. As well as our own pets, we love to photograph our clients' pets too.

LAPOLLA, LOU
My photograph was taken at approximately 7:45 A.M. near a small town called Bush in Louisiana. I travel the back roads sometimes in my work as a residential and commercial construction repair contractor. I take my camera from time to time along with me as I travel some of the back country roads here in Tennessee. Many of my photographs are taken in the morning or late afternoon when the light can be used to control the contrast of my work.

LARIMORE, PATRICIA
I took this picture while attending the Navy-Rutgers game in Annapolis. The flyby was so awesome. I wanted to capture it. I was afraid it wouldn't turn out because I was shooting into the sun. What a pleasant surprise when the print was developed!

LAUGHERY, NANCY J.
I have had a love affair with photography for over twenty years, and I have thousands of photographs to prove it. I love to look through the lens of a camera and capture that particular moment in time forever on film. "A Freeze Frame Of Love" was taken on a Cape Cod beach at sunset while we were on vacation. It was a special moment between a mother and her child that will never be captured in quite the same way again. It portrays the special bond between a mother and child that we can only hope will last forever.

LAYTON, ROBERT R.
My wife and I have lived in Milton for thirty years. I taught Carol to drive. We are owner-operators and ran as a team, until she retired in November 1996. When we bought Lilly, she went everywhere with us. From the time she was a puppy and to his day, she loves going. We never put her up to the steering wheel. When she wants

to drive, she just jumps up and puts her feet on the wheel. Carol took this picture going west on I-80 in Pennsylvania. After forty years of driving, I'm retiring at the end of March.

LEACH, CURTIS J.
This photo was taken while downtown shopping the day after Thanksgiving. I brought my camera to take some pictures of the holiday decorations. I was sitting and resting in front of the art museum. I thought the lion with the big wreath and bow would be a nice picture to take.

LEACH, HARRIET
The beauty of the Australian sky is indescribable. If you wait and watch the sun sink, there is a moment when both the Earth and the Heavens glow with the same ruddy light. The actual name of this sculpture is *Bajo El Sol Jaguar*, and it can be found at Broken Hill, New South Wales, Australia. It is based on the legend of the sun and moon where the jaguar opens his mouth to protect the sun through the night.

LEACH, KOLI
This is a picture of my dog, Manna, droopy-eyed and fighting to stay awake. I got Manna when she was only eight weeks old. Every day since then, she has made me laugh with the crazy things she does—lying on her back and growling wildly at her tail, crunching on her favorite treat of raw carrots, and banging her tail against everything when I come home. Manna is so loving, free to be who she is, uninhibited, and showing of all her emotions with nothing to hide.

LEE, SAM R.
The contrasting outline of the trumpeting angels atop this local church spire presents a great opportunity for sunset photography. All that's required of the photographer is cooperation from the weather and patience for the right moment of color and light. This setting offers great potential for aspiring photographers to produce consistent, pleasing photographs.

LEEPER, MARY ELLEN
Taking this photo, I was unaware that the falls appeared to be falling on the cab of the pickup. I do not take photos often, but this one always held a soft spot in my heart. Now with my husband gone, what a wonderful surprise it is to receive word this has been accepted by the International Library of Photography for publication.

LEIGHTON, JENNIFER
My niece, Julia, was twenty months old when I took this photo. She is admiring the beautiful flower garden, which had been planted by her grandfather, who was called Poppy. Poppy passed away the previous winter, but his flower garden remains a true legacy.

LEONHARD, JACQUELINE
An Oklahoma native, I'm eighty-four and a retired news reporter/PR consultant with a passion for family and photography. My late husband, Jim, and I lived in Sweden when we met Edwin and the late Margaret Reid, "Irish Boy's" grandparents. Visiting the Reids in England recently, I took this picture of Lawrence. (Earlier, he had

pulled a pot of boiling water off the range over his face, but was miraculously unscarred.) In my cottage adjoining the home of my daughter and her husband, Jamie and Bob Haeuser, is my "gallery." My entire kitchen wall is covered with family photos, the oldest of which is of my great-great-grandfather, born in 1797 in New York State, who trekked west to the Ozarks as a country doctor; the youngest is Clarissa, four years old, my great-granddaughter, who lives in Oregon.

LEROY, EDWARD J.
This is a picture of Buddy, our bichon frise who we adopted from the Bichon Rescue Society. He is our best friend and constant companion. Other than sunbathing, his two favorite pastimes are imitating famous movie stars and having his picture taken.

LEVENSON, LESLIE M.
I have been (and am still) known as the "camera-crazy lady" by my family for most of my life. This photo, which happened to be the very last exposure on my roll of film, was taken near Fountain Hill, AZ. It captures the expansive view of the giant saguaro cactus along with red rocks, desert plants, and weather, which completes the scene at the right moment. My husband, Paul, and I go to Arizona quite often to appreciate the beauty of the magnificent surroundings, which everyone should see!

LEWIS, MARLENE
Squirt is a lovable cat, especially in the morning. She grew up with her owners, not her brothers or sisters. We found her at six ounces and about one-and-a-half weeks old. She had no voice, no teeth, and her eyes barely opened. She was abandoned. We bottle-fed her until she was six weeks old. She is the alarm clock in the morning, which of course is feeding time for her. If I don't wake up, she pulls my hair with her teeth. Now she does help her mother on occasion, being noisy. She travels by car or plane on most vacations, but she's always glad to get home. That is her place of authority.

LIBMAN, MITCHEL
"Rain Dance" was our pet for a short time while we stayed at an animal sanctuary for a few days during a short photography vacation. My wife, Marilyn, and I found "Rain Dance" to be very photogenic and a joy to be with. Photography had been my hobby for many years, and most of our vacations are planned with taking pictures in mind. Both my granddaughters, Casey and Nikki Haimes, are successful child models, and their mother, Gail, is a world champion country western dancer. My son-in-law is a five time world champion offshore boat racer, and my son, Wayne, is an entertainer. All of that good fortune gives me many opportunities for wonderful photography.

LIDGARD, LISA A.
My family and I were on vacation in Arkansas, and after a fun-filled day of sight-seeing, we decided to sit on our balcony and enjoy the beautiful sunset. It was one of the most beautiful sunsets we had ever seen.

LINDSEY, ROBERT A.
"Presidential Turmoil" was shot in July 2000 while we were vacationing in South Dakota. A very harsh storm came up while we were waiting for the evening lighting ceremony of the memorial. The name for the photograph was derived from the past electoral process between Bush and Gore. I could just imagine past presidents turning over in their graves, with all the counts, recounts, and accusations of impropriety. Although my last three years of employment were as a billboard advertising photographer, I am strictly an amateur doing my own thing. The photo of myself was even done with a timer.

LONG, RITA W.
My boyfriend, Tony, insisted I send this photo since it's his favorite. Who knew it would have been selected for publication in *Vivid Exposures*? This is a picture of my first dog, a Pembroke Welsh corgi, named Master Foojie. He was fourteen weeks old and not quite ready for the stairs. I would try to convince him to leave the house by saying, "Come out, come out, wherever you are!", and out would pop this cute little head with a big smile. I love trying to capture his expressions on film. Since then, peek-a-boo is still one of his favorite games.

LOUGHRY, DONALD F.
I am a science teacher from central Kentucky, and I consider myself a wildflower buff. While driving down one of those endless Kentucky country roads in late spring, I looked to my left and was struck by this snowy field of dandelions. Talk about being in the right place at the right time! The day after I took the photo, it was rainy and windy. It's too bad. Some of the best things in life can be blown away in an instant.

LOY, MICHELLE
In 1997, a very special feline of mine died. I was left with only a few blurred photos of an animal who I spent so many hours with, and I vowed from then on to photograph my cat friends whenever I had the chance. Thus, my passion for photography grew. I found myself more observant of their beauty in all forms, those plump with time, the homeless stray, the long-haired lady, the fearless tomcat—felines of all colors, origins, and personalities. The photos, as well as my affections, have been completely captured by the mystical, untamed soul of the feline.

LYLES, IDA B.
Thank you very much for choosing my photograph for publication. I'm so excited. I can hardly write. I took the picture outside my front door one evening after a brief thunderstorm. I went to the door and looked up. Lo and behold, a "Kodak moment" was there. The whole picture was over in a moment.

LYONS, KATHLEEN A.
I try to see the world through the lens of my camera. Therefore, most of the photos that I take are informal and not posed. This photo was taken during a family reunion in Wisconsin. When I heard the familiar plunk of an object landing in water, I turned to find Ryan pitching rocks into the pond. I was able to get two shots before he lost

interest. I think that the photo captures the anticipation of the moment and evokes memories of a popular childhood activity. Yet it also exhibits a sense of peace, harmony, and balance between nature and its inhabitants.

MAADANJIAN, HOURIK
I remember telling the tour bus driver as I was looking at the reflection of the clouds and the mountains on the lake that this would be a one million dollar shot. He smiled and said, "I know; that's why I brought you here." I am glad he did because this stop was not part of the tour, and it was the most beautiful scenery I had ever seen. I thank him for sharing this beautiful scenery with us, and I would like to thank my father for teaching and showing me the beauty of nature through the eyes of the camera.

MACIOCE, ALEXANDER
I was on a trip at the Bronx Zoo, when I spotted this little bee on this beautiful flower. I'm glad I can share this photo with the world.

MacMILLAN, ANN S.
This is a photograph of my granddaughter, Holli, and Holmes. For a two-year-old, there are fun days at the park and then there are those serious days! Holli's brother, Luke, and I decided to go to the Estes Park, Colorado, playground, and Holli had a two-year-old attitude that day. I snapped the photo in the late afternoon, with the sun setting over Rocky Mountain National Park. The sunlight, color, and expression made a delightful photo. I used a 35mm Canon Eos Rebel X and 200 Kodak film.

MADSON, LINDA R.
Our son, Stacy, works for the Padlock Ranch out of Dayton, WY. He obviously has a sense of humor. He found this rock on a hill near his home and thought it looked like it needed a pair of jeans to wear. It is located near his patio as you enter the house. My husband and I had a good laugh. He says nobody can go by it without doing a double take, then smiling and asking where he found that rock. It is definitely a conversation piece.

MANSFIELD, RAYMOND
I photographed Urquhart Castle ruins when I, my wife, Delia, our daughter, Debbie, and her husband, Steve, visited the west coast of Scotland in October 2000. The ruins overlook Loch Ness, where the famous monster was supposedly sited in years past. The lake is so calm that anything surfacing, near or far, could be easily noticed. Perhaps the couple in this photo were watching for such an event. Does not the castle pose an intriguing site against the Scottish landscape? Such a scene can make one wonder what it was like when the castle was in its prime.

MANSHP, NOLA
Sometimes you look at a picture, and it just takes your breath away. That's what this one did to me. These are just three of my five grandchildren: Tanner, Ross, and Alexis. I work in a juvenile home, and when I look at this picture of innocence, I wish the very best for them and know they have good parents who will do their best at guiding them through the trying years of youth.

My only regret is that Hunter and Jordyn weren't visiting this day, as they could have made Grandma's sunshine complete.

MARGOLIN, FELIX
Traveling is my passion. The first thing I wanted to see in Paris was the world-famous Eiffel Tower. I still keep my drawings of it from the time I was a fourth grader. I believe this iron tower has its own soul. Just imagine how many people and events of the twentieth century it has witnessed! I stood there for several hours, admiring the architecture and observing day slipping into night. Finally, on the ground I took this last shot to preserve the beautiful Eiffel creation, not only for my memory, but also to share it with all of you.

MARTIN, DOROTHY G.
Southeastern Oklahoma has miles of scenic beauty. Whatever the season, there are vast opportunities to capture and take home a memory. Because I live here, the only effort needed is to walk outdoors. That day—feeling depressed—I didn't want to go there. It was almost sundown. In this area snow doesn't stay very long. Where's my coat and camera? Wow! What a bright focus for a gloomy mood. Days later with photo in hand, much to my surprise, I had caught a rainbow! Green grass will grow again; sadness will disappear.

MASON, DAVID E.
I'm David Mason, a native to Butte, MT. Like many people, my camera is always with me, waiting for that once-in-a-lifetime shot. I took this unique sunset shot in my front yard. It was during the fires of 2000. Between Mother Nature and God I was able to capture this beautiful moment in time. I love to take pictures of the natural beauty God made for us to enjoy. I put a lot of feeling into my photos, or so I've been told by people. That pleases me to know. Put a camera in my hand, turn me loose in the mountains, and I'm "happier than a gopher in loose dirt."

MATTHEWS, ROBERTA
This photo is of my two-year-old granddaughter carrying green onions from my parents' house.

MAURER, LISA
This is a photo of Hailey Jeannine, our daughter. Hailey, born on Christmas Day, was eighteen months old and quick to catch on to one of my favorite pastimes—gardening. My husband, Paul, and I have two other daughters, Chelsea and Melanie. We live in a beautiful rural area with views of the Catskill Mountains, and we share our home with three dogs, six cats, and eleven rabbits. So we have plenty of photo opportunities!

MAYER, KATHERINE
This is a photo of my roommate. I took this photo as part of a biography assignment, as it illustrates her outlook on life. I think her expression and pose convey the title. I think it came out great!

MAYER, LESLIE S.
As our family gathers for this very important day, we steal a moment away from the crowd. I have never been more proud of my niece, Kimberly, than on this very day. She's a dream come true, a

vision in white. She's so beautiful, pondering the life ahead of her, knowing she is leaving behind Daddy's little girl.

McCLUSKEY, ROBYN
This is a photo of two gray whales snacking in the bay. One whale had just come up for a breath of fresh air (you can see its blow), while another whale was diving and showing its tail. I took this picture while vacationing with my family on the northern Oregon coast. We had stopped at a scenic lookout point and were fortunate to see a small pod of whales. I was walking along the bluffs when I spotted the whales feeding. I was so excited. We are lucky to share our Earth with these amazing animals.

McCOLLUM, TERRAN
This is a picture of Jesse and Rusty, our miniature Doberman pinschers. My husband, Willis, and I are truly amazed on a daily basis at what enjoyment and comic relief these two bring us!

McDANIEL, H. C.
This is a picture of Cades Cove, TN. It was taken from Rich Mountain Road. My mother was born April 29, 1916, in Cades Cove. Cades Cove holds great memories and sentiments of my family and their heritage. Russell Gregory, the founder of Gregory's Bald, was my third great-grandfather. He moved his family into Cades Cove and herded his cattle to and from Cades Cove and Gregory's Bald according to the seasons. The Gregories also had a secret cave inside Cades Cove. Cades Cove holds many great family heritages.

McDONALD, LACITA A.
A waterfall of ice? Actually, it is ages and ages of mineral deposits at the base of Mammoth Springs in Wyoming's beautiful Yellowstone National Park. My husband, Bobby, and I are Oklahoma factory workers. Getting away on our yearly vacation is something we both look forward to. I love taking photographs, Bobby loves NASCAR, and we both love nature's beauty. Visit Yellowstone; its magnificent beauty is breathtaking and picture-perfect.

McLAUGHLIN, BECKY
This is a photo of my sister, Andrea. We were en route to Denali National Park in Alaska on a train. I was trying for the perfect mountain image. The sun was bright, and I caught my sister's reflection. She was obviously deep in thought. When I look at this photo I visit beautiful Alaska all over again.

McLEAN, SANDRA
Here is a potential employee for the department of corrections, my granddaughter, Courtney, age four, with my dog, Dixie. I made her outfit for her so she could pretend to be a correctional officer like me. We enjoy picture-taking and spending time together. I can show off my granddaughter, my dog, and my hobby.

McPHAIL, RACHAEL
This is a photo of my beloved dog, Ginger, that I got when I was nine. I don't know her age, but I think she was three then and is four now. I got her from the Santa Barbara Animal Shelter, where she spent three months. I have very few clues to her

271

history. My only estimate to her pedigree is that she is half Queensland heeler, a quarter Cardigan Welsh corgi, and a quarter Lab. Despite the fact that she was badly abused, she is sweet, kind, and loving and pulls me on my scooter.

MEFFORD, JEAN
This wee fairy often visits our garden disguised as our two-year-old granddaughter, MacKenzie. Imagine her surprise when I caught her one evening among the flowers dressed as herself, wings and all! Surprising fairies and capturing our grandchildren, MacKenzie and Wyatt, on film are two of my favorite pastimes.

MENDONCA, TAMMY
I have always been a fan of photographers that could catch those special moments that were not expected. This is a picture of my three-year-old daughter, Kelsey, and our black Arabian stallion, RA Otar Rudan. They are always so fascinated with each other. She loves giving him kisses, and he loves her around like a puppy dog. Fortunately, I caught it on film.

MESSIER, JUDITH
Nikia is a Vermont-born, New Hampshire resident Siberian husky who loves to play at the ocean. She is very intelligent. She loves to be photographed, and I would say she's a natural! Nikia is very endearing to our family. She was named by our children, Laura and Nickolas. Steve and I braved a Vermont snowstorm to pick her up at the Serendipity Kennels, and she is worth every inch of snow that fell in our path. Nikia is a wonderful companion and has brought so much joy to our family. We always hope to give her the good life she deserves!

METZ GRACE, SUSIE
A "Maui Moment" by the sea left nothing to be desired for newlyweds on their honeymoon. As the sun set over the Pacific, the torches were lit, signaling the start of a feast—the Old Lahaina Luau. Exotic dancing, beating drums, and Hawaiian food delighted our every sense. We debated which element was more spectacular. Was it the sunset, the show, or the dining? In conclusion, we agreed that each portion of the setting was equally impressive, but the most spectacular element of all was the feeling of closeness, contentment, and passion—the true love shared between us. Aloha!

MEYER, ANDREW
This photo was taken off the coast of Key West, FL, in the summer of 1998. I sat on a boat for what seemed like eternity just waiting for the perfect moment. Right now, I'm fifteen and a sophomore in high school. I play a lot of sports, such as football and wrestling. I'm also very active in my church. I recently started to enjoy the arts, and I wish to pursue that interest. I hope you can enjoy the picture as much as I do.

MILLER, LISA A.
I have been inspired to travel by simply seeing a picture in a book. When I reach my destination I find that the experience exceeds my expectations. Moorea is an exotic paradise in French Polynesia

near Tahiti. Spending my honeymoon there was a magical experience that will be hard to top.

MILLER, MARIAN L.
This is my dog, Kippy. She is a two-year-old cocker spaniel/golden retriever mix, an adoptee from our local shelter. In fact, she is a graduate of Rover Rehab, a cooperative program between the shelter and the nearby county correctional institution. Certain dogs are selected from the shelter to be trained by prison inmates to make them more easily adoptable as they are house-broken and trained to answer to certain commands. I am a retired teacher and find Kippy my most photogenic and loving companion.

MILLER, MARY
Mary Miller's prayers were answered October 7, 2000. It was an evening in the woods not to be forgotten. Other times I would be entertained with chipmunks, birds, and squirrels, but this evening was windy with nothing about. I was about to quit when I spied this seven-point. He came my way and stopped with his head behind a big tree, twenty yards out. That's when I shot it. It went down in this lovely wooded area—my first deer with the bow and arrow at age fifty-eight.

MILLER, MICHELE
Six hours southwest from Denver is some of the most beautiful scenery I've ever encountered. My daughter, Marina, and I love taking road trips. The views we witness in this area are breathtaking. I visit these mountains and others many times in the summer and fall to capture the beauty of each season. Although I reside in Denver, part of my heart is always here.

MILLER, REGINA
Photography has always been one of my passions. I'm the shutterbug at all the family events. I combine my passion with my favorite hobby, scrapbooking and preserving my family's memories for future generations. My husband and I visited Kauai for our fifth anniversary. This photo was taken from a helicopter tour we took while exploring the island.

MIRACLE, MICHELLE
Our pet hamster was out roaming the house and found our dog's bowl. Inside was the dog's treat, Golden Grahams cereal, with no milk. My daughter, Roxanne, named him Tato because his red eyes reminded her of a tomato. Tato was well trained. He seemed to know when he was being photographed. Now sending this, my eyes fill with tears, for our Tato has now passed away at five years old. He was my baby boy!

MOHLER, MARY K.
James Everett Mohler, my husband of fifty years, was issued the foot locker (right background) in April of 1942 at McDill Field, Florida. For three-and-one-half years the two were constant companions, going from McDill Field, Tampa, FL, to England, France, and Belgium. The memorabilia and foot locker are now fifty-nine years old. On December 28, 1999, Wesley Fawcett from Zuni, VA, and Trevor Fawcett from Basalt, CO, were spending Christmas in Ohio. James Mohler said, "Come look at my foot locker." While the three

were digging into the locker, like digging for gold, they came to the three flight helmets; thus the photo. February 17, 2001, will be our fiftieth anniversary. *Vivid Exposures* will be a belated anniversary present for James.

MOONEY, ERICA
"Face To Face With Fall" captures my two cousins' love for life. Here Daniel and Aaron are seen doing what they do best—being little boys. I play volleyball, tennis, and the piano, and I'm an actress. However, my favorite title remains young photographer. I enjoy traveling and taking photos wherever I go. Besides, film is far less expensive than a lost memory.

MOORE, LYNNE M.
This was taken on a beautiful summer day a few years ago. My great-nephew was enjoying his pool when he noticed my year-old Saint, Sinbad, was looking at him. He waddled over to him and gave the big puppy a kiss. Sinbad and Cameron are close in age; now at four, they are buddies.

MORGAN, JUNE
For as long as I can remember, I have been fascinated by photographs and photography. I titled this photo "Memories" for two reasons: it was taken while on a walk in the country with a friend I have known since childhood, and when I saw this old home, it tugged at my heart. Thinking of all the memories this house must hold, I wondered who had left the bike just where it was. So the walk and the house created wonderful memories.

MORRIS, VIRGINIA L.
Taking photos is my passion. A retired medical research associate, my camera is always at my side. Shown here are two of my favorite subjects—my son, Nicholas, and my granddaughter, Tabitha. This photo was taken on a warm spring day in early June of 1999. Nick was ten, and Tabitha was seven years old. We had just moved to the country, and Nick and Tabitha were feeling as free as the breeze that day.

MORROW, DONNA
I've always loved polar bears, and this was my first opportunity to see them live in their natural surroundings. It was my first trip to Alaska, with Barrow being the best area to view these beautiful creatures. I love taking photos, and animals in nature offer many different, unique opportunities. I hope to learn more by taking classes and practicing. And by the way, it was twenty degrees below zero!

MORROW, KIMBERLY
This photograph of Zeus was taken when he was about eight months old. Zeus is a shar-pei. He doesn't like to wear clothes, but he did agree to pose for this adorable picture. I used to think dogs were too much responsibility, but along with the additional responsibility comes a lot of joy. Zeus has changed my life for the better. Zeus is three now. We love him as if he was our child, and we dress him that way too! We look forward to many more years of love and photographs with Zeus.

MOZES, MELODY
This is one of my favorite spur-of-the-moment

shots. Most of the photos I have of Houdini are blurs as he pins me to the ground, slobbering me with kisses and drool. On one of our walks in my woods, I almost forgot I had the camera when Houdini took this regal stance. I clicked, then he jumped off the wood pile, branches flying everywhere, and pinned me against a tree, once again kissing and slobbering my face with that big grin he has, as if to say, "Did I do good, Mom?" I love this guy; he's my bud.

MURPHY, PHOTOGRAPHER
This picture was taken in London during the summer of 2000. The moment I developed this, I asked myself, "Now, how did that come out so well?", because I had no idea I was capable of taking such a beautiful photograph. That's just it though. Anyone can take a picture; it's what you put into it that lasts forever. I hope everyone enjoys this image captured on film for years to come.

NAGY, SANDY
Lady was my first dog and best friend. This picture was taken after a study break when she was helping by "holding" my glasses. Even after the picture was taken, she always found a place to relax close to me, so when I took off my glasses she could wear them as a symbol of our close friendship and affection.

NEELY, SANDRA
I love the beach. I also love photography! Every trip I make to the coast of North or South Carolina, I always take photos of the sun rising. During some of my early morning photo shoots, my husband, Roy Neely, my mother, Thelma Baker, my sisters, Shirley Dunevant and Pat Wrightenberry, and my friend, Janet Jones, have kept me company waiting for the sun to shine. This particular shot is a favorite of mine, especially since it favors a sun setting. The seagull is the added touch—serene and peaceful.

NELSON, PATRICE
Once in a while, a photo has the power to bring you right back to a perfect moment in a great day we all shared together. The true gift is that every time you look at that shot you feel good all over again! That's what I try and go for when taking pictures of people I love. My husband, Jeff, was the shutterbug before the babies came. Now it's not unusual for me to use a whole roll of film on the kids—LaNaya, Casey, and Mitchell—during the day, an afternoon, or even an activity.

NICHOLS, KATHI
I took this photo on my first trip to Lake Cumberland. It was mid-July, and everything was picture-perfect. There was such a peaceful feeling about the lake.

NOLAN, JAMES
Last October my wife, Karen, and I took a ride on a Sunday afternoon to enjoy the fall foliage. This picture was taken at a small lake in Granville, MA, which is very close to our home in Gronby, CT.

NORELL, NICHOLE
It was a cool autumn day when I took the picture and fantasized of stories I will tell someday when

I gain some sort of small recognition for doing something I adore—photographing all for which I am grateful. In dreams I would have dove in fully clothed, let the water surround me, slipped off my socks and shoes, and made my way to the gazebo hidden around the island bend waiting for the sun to set. Only when my mother calls me home will I finally leave from my post. All at once, as I extend my arms and legs to begin my journey home, I feel the water, and "In Dreams" I awake.

O'FARRELL, KEVIN
This is our granddaughter, Samantha. She enjoys being in our garden working with the flowers and plants, as is obvious in the photo. While deadheading the rhodos, I went to get a container for the spent blooms. Upon returning, lo and behold there was Samantha on the ladder smiling through the flowers, eager and ready to help. When I saw the expression on her face amidst the flowers, I wanted to capture it on film and share it with others. Photography is one of my favorite hobbies—always has been and always will be. It is a hobby you can do for your entire lifetime.

OLIVER, DOROTHY
I am an eighty-one-year-old great-grandmother. This picture is of our daughter, her daughter, and her grandson. Photography has fascinated me for years. It has always been my hobby. I am a minister's wife, and I always look for beautiful and unusual things in God's creations to photograph. I always take my camera with me, even to church.

OLIVER, EDUARDO
I only take pictures on special occasions. I have visited my brother-in-law in the city of Palm Coast many times. A tranquil river runs behind their house. In one of my visits, I noticed the clearest water I have ever seen. Something inside told me to take pictures of the unique view. I took various shots. I have never seen the same beautiful reflection of my relative's home again. The last picture I took showed many large fish swimming happily in the crystal waters of the reflection of "My House By The Lake."

OLIVER, SANDRA L.
I have always enjoyed amateur photography, as it offers such vast varieties of treasures. Nature's beauty, like a kaleidoscope, never repeats itself, only to be more beautiful with a blink of the eye. It's a gift to us through the seasons, so I captured this as another moment in life. Not everyone has the privilege of this beauty, so I chose to share it with others.

OLIVER, SUSAN M.
I have been a shutterbug since I was young, and among my family and friends I'm always the one with the camera documenting get-togethers and what not. It had been a very long and dreary winter in New Hampshire, and my friend and I were taking a drive when winter had finally thawed. Lo and behold, we came around a corner on a country road, and there it was; the triumph of spring had come!

OSBORNE, NORM
This photo, "Reflections," was taken at Twin Lakes, California, which is located on the back

side of Yosemite. There is more to this collection, which is a gem. I enjoy sharing this and other photos I've taken.

OSTRANDER, GERALD P.
I am a technician for a company in Allentown, PA, that is a distributor of one-hour photo lab equipment. My wife and I enjoy traveling and taking pictures of the beauty that surrounds us. We try to capture that beauty on film. This picture is a result of one of our excursions. It is one of the many waterfalls in an area about one hour from our home in Pennsylvania. It's in a little town in the Poconos called Bushkill. The falls are known as the Niagara of Pennsylvania.

OTTO, JAMES
This is a photo of my husband, James, and our senecal parrot, Odie. This is his favorite place to ride when we go hunting or camping.

PANAKKAL, DILIP
Lost in the mountains of the mystical Sultanate of Oman, the "Fire Mountain" was our last ray of hope. Literally we had missed a turn on our off-road trip, and we finally found a blacktop road. Our relief was reflected in this spectacular display. A British group did not survive flash floods on the same route the very next week. This photo reminds me of that tragedy, and I thank God we are alive.

PARQUET, THEO
We were baby-sitting our granddaughter, Larissa Jade. We laid her down on a Disney blanket and took her picture. It was not 'til the photo was developed that we noticed she had Mickey ears. Hence the title, "Our Little Mouse."

PARSONS, SCOTT
Bailey is the first pet that Shelby and I have had together. To tell you the truth, we have both taken so many pictures of him growing up that we aren't really sure which one of us took this particular picture. What we do know is that our love for him and each other makes it a great memory of when he was a little pup.

PASCHAL, DAVID
I stopped to get something to eat. I had a camera half-full of film, so I started taking shots. I saw the train and its location and shot. The picture, "A Meeting Place," was developed. I like taking pictures, especially if they say something to me, and this one has.

PATON, MICHAEL
"Hanging Lake" is a photograph taken in Glenwood Springs, CO. About an hour hike, the lake is in a flat area among several cliffs. The two little girls are unknown to me—sisters, I believe, that were playing on the log that juts out into the crystal clear pool of water. This timeless image was taken on Kodak high speed infrared film with a Nikon F100. I see the image as timeless because there is nothing to date it, and it could have been taken anywhere in the world.

PATTERSON, STACEY
My husband, Ryan, my true inspiration for this photo, and I were on our first vacation as a mar-

ried couple in New York this past fall when we happened upon the New York Stock Exchange. After discussing our hopes and dreams for our new future together and realizing the failures and success stories people put into the stock market each day, we noticed this homeless man staring aimlessly at the idealistic building. We thought it was the perfect picture of today's society: while some may gain enormous amounts of wealth, others will always remain on the outside looking in.

PAVLICH, CAROL ANN
My picture was taken from a canoe on a weekend outing on the backwaters of the Ogeechee River near Midville, GA. The uniqueness of this photo is that when you turn this picture sideways all sorts of imaginary things come into view.

PELLETIER, CAROLYN
Sunday evening, my six-year-old son, Sean, was running along the beautifully colored ocean shore. He was so joyous since he had just been to church, and he looked like he was in such a lovable mood. The Lord recognized his goodness and faithfulness and laid His light upon my son's head. It was such a humble sight to see my son sharing this moment with a stranger he was playing with. He had his eyes closed with delight from the beautiful view of his first beach on Easton Street in Newport, RI. I treasure this picture because of the beautiful sight it captured. This is proof of why I truly believe my son, Sean, is a gift from God.

PELTZER, CARRIE
A little paint transformed my pregnant belly into "Our Little Pumpkin," a unique gift for my husband who has a special appreciation because he is a pumpkin farmer. He could not believe his eyes. We laughed for days!

PENTECOST, PAT
Copper, our beloved Yorkshire terrier and master of his domain, sniffed with unmistakable hauteur. When there was no response from our brand new granddaughter, Sarah, save wide-eyed wonder, Copper pawed the rug and moved in closer. And that's when they met nose-to-nose. Copper poked Sarah. She poked him back. They were friends ever after. I am not one for taking pictures, except when there comes a time that I want very much to remember.

PEREIRA, LYDIA
Sewing is my favorite hobby, and my daughter likes to model dresses. I take pictures for memories. She loves those moments. We like to choose natural scenery—beaches, flowers, and green grass—for our pictures. Taking photos is my second pastime, and we enjoy it together. I won my first camera in 1993 in a contest. Now I have a better camera that my husband gave to me. I am always looking to capture great moments. I'm a student in the Parent Power Program in Florida, and I wish to be a professional photographer in the future.

PEREZ, B. J.
The sweet spirit that flows amongst the humble worshippers in this church produces the most amazing peace that one could imagine. The precious souls who gather there are the richest people

in all the world. I became acquainted with them on a missionary trip. They grabbed my heart. I returned to their country and married a native Cuban, who will join me here one day. I have established several meaningful friendships that will last a lifetime. I have learned so much from them and will never take overabundance of food and material things for granted again.

PERRY, SHERRIE L.
I came from a family of picture-takers. I've been taking pictures for many years and would love for my profession to be behind a lens. This picture was taken at Weekapaug Point, RI. I waited several minutes until the wave action hit the rock at the right time.

PHELAN, CARRIE
I began to enjoy photography as a way to share the four beautiful seasons of New England with family in Texas. I send them photos of the foliage, snow, mountains, and oceans. Photography for me is a way to capture the beauty that life has to offer. I carry my camera with me wherever I go, because I know at any moment I may capture something beautiful forever.

PHELPS, JOHN H., JR.
This is my dog, Gypsy, a golden Lab and setter mix. Her thing was to run on the beach. While running, she would look from side to side as to see where the competition was. In this picture she was running on water and sand and was actually trying to outrun her shadow and reflection, which she thought were other dogs. Photography is just a hobby with me. I love having the power to freeze time and memories. Mirror images, my favorite.

PILETTE, MARY ANNE
Our family enjoys whistles, kazoos, horns, blowouts, and more. At this birthday party, several members tried to see who could blow the longest. They kept trying to do it over and over. It was not a staged photo. They could hardly keep from laughing.

PILLOW, TRACY SANFORD
Being married to a soldier and raising four (soon to be five) kids keeps my life pretty interesting. I keep journals of our adventures, and I'm always snapping pictures. This is a photo I took while on an amazing trip with Molt International Children's Services to work in an orphanage in Delhi. I will never forget the little ones I held and rocked and the hopelessness I've seen, felt, and heard. I will never forget the India I experienced because the eyes and smiles of the kids traveled home with me, in my heart . . .

POLAK, MELODY M.
Well, here she is . . . "Our Lovable Bunny," Amber Meaghan Stewart. She is our first and only child. She is our miracle child that wasn't ever expected to be. As you can see by her smile, she is a most welcome addition.

POLAND, CAROL J.
The little girl in this photograph is Annie Freeman, daughter of Curt and Crickett of Moorefield, WV. She and I met February 22,

1995, five hours after Annie was born. Today we share a special friendship, one that is bound by heart strings and will last a lifetime. This photo was taken on River Road in Fisher, WV, at the home of Carol and Preston Poland who fixed the house up after the '85 flood. We have lived there for fourteen years. We have one daughter, Jennifer Whetzel, who is married to Fred Whetzel of Moorefield, WV.

POST, SANDRA
This picture is from one of ten rolls of film taken during my ten-day Alaskan tour. Each picture could have been named "Mother Nature At Her Best." This photo was taken en route to White Pass Summit via the White Pass and Yukon Route passenger train, leaving Skagway, AK, and climbing 2,865 feet on the narrow gauge railroad built one hundred years ago (1898 - 1899) during the Klondike gold rush. It's also known as the "scenic railway of the world." I would encourage anyone to take an Alaskan tour, to see the ice glaciers, wildlife, floral gardens, snow covered mountains, the peaceful cruise, and much more.

PRICE, JILL ANN
Sage has been a wonderful addition to our family. Along with our ragdoll, Sebastian, they both have added so much entertainment and love to my son, Michael, my husband, Mike's, and my lives. Can you believe this adorable kitten was a stray? I can't imagine what would have happened had we not brought him into our home. I've always thought people should take responsibility for their animals! It makes me sad to think of all the strays that don't find a loving home. I'm so thankful for the day Sage wandered into our hearts!

PUCKETT, ANGELA
My husband and I were out riding around passing the time away. We saw this baby fawn cross the road, so we were watching it. I just happened to turn my head, and there she was just standing there watching her fawn. I got my camera and took the picture. I don't think she knew we could see her. So when I got my picture back, all I said was, "I did see you."

QUIMBY, ERIC
Topography buffs, take heed. If climbing mountains, rolling over steep trestles bisecting cities, and skirting edges of rivers sounds picturesque, then Amtrak's "empire builder" is your ticket. On the flipside of this beautiful day in Montana, my family, living near Philadelphia, was getting pounded by Hurricane Floyd in September of 1999. As my children get older and move about the United States of America, I find my fatherhood and photography roles adapting to accommodate new situations. I click less human subjects and more "machinery in the outdoors" shots.

RACINE, BARBARA ANN
The day we brought Kaylee home, we knew she was going to be a character. Kaylee has an older sister, Casey, whom she loves to torment dearly. When Casey decides to lash back with all of her eighty-five pounds, Kaylee runs for shelter. So Kaylee decided that the coffee table would be her safest bet. Well, Kaylee liked it so much that she

decided that it would also be her favorite place to "Rest For A Spell" and re-energize herself.

RAE, RICHARD
My wife, Judy, and I live in Folsom, CA, about twenty-four miles from Sacramento. A retired state civil service employee, my interests are photography, surfing the internet, and square dancing. I often carry my point-and-shoot Pentax camera when I go out. It is ready for the quirky situations we run into unexpectedly, as in the case of this restaurant sign in Folsom. How could I resist a shot like that? It's the kind of "take you by surprise" scene I like to look for when I go anywhere.

RAPP, KATHY
Here is four-year-old Lindsay with her eighty-four-year-old grandfather. Although he is teaching her how to fish in the backyard pond, the real life lesson here consists of unqualified love. The lesson is taught in two ways: a child's unconditional love for her grandfather and the grandfather's gift of love for his young granddaughter.

RATLIFF, MARILYN K.
While vacationing in Tennessee last fall, I was intrigued by this stream off the beaten tourist path. What a pleasure and thrill it was to find it and to spend a little time away from business in one of God's cathedrals. I've also had the privilege of being associated with a water company for the past sixteen years, and I realize the impact that water can have in each of our lives.

REED, BRIAN
My picture was taken on a family vacation last year. I look for unique and spontaneous shots, which is reflected in the rare beauty of the deer shown in the photograph. There are many natural beauties in the world waiting to be captured by the lens of a camera. This is my goal when I aim at something that catches my eye. Often, people ask me to take pictures of extracurricular events that my children and their children participate in. It gives me pleasure to make people happy.

REED, DELEMA T.
I keep my camera with me at all times. You never know when you could have that special "Kodak moment." I was on my way home from my son's last fall. The foliage was so beautiful I couldn't pass it up. I can look at this picture, and my mind can take me anywhere I want to go . . . to my parents' home when I was a child or to places where I raised my children . . . or in the twilight of life, to my Heavenly home, just around that next curve. Let your mind take you home.

REEVES, TOM
The black-and-white mix breed, Sebastian, and the shar-pei, Gummy, were both unwanted dogs. They were rescued by Leslie White and taken home to join two other outcasts, along with two cats she has saved. She can't stand to see any animal mistreated, taking in as many as possible and finding homes for others. Her household consists of Gummy, Sebastian, Major, and Cinnamon, plus two cats, Gismo and Baxter. I get to hang around as someone to lie on, play with, and sometimes use as a chew toy.

RESPICIO, MARIA
Like most kids I know, my son, Jason, loves to take nice, warm baths. I would usually put up his wet hair and let it go in different directions. When this was taken, I told Jason he was a shark, and to my surprise, he just posed and looked real mean and yet so adorably cute. This is indeed a precious moment. I am so glad I was able to capture it on film and share this with everyone.

REYNOLDS, LORI
This photo was taken during my family's first trip together after my mother was diagnosed with cancer. On the way to Lake Tahoe from New York, we stopped in Las Vegas to catch up with my older brother. While everyone else took in the casinos, glitzy shows, and buffets, I stole away some much-needed time to myself and watched the outdoor dolphin show. It was a wonderful trip, and even more wonderful was the news last week that my mother's cancer is gone!

RIDGWAY, SANDY
This photo was taken at a zoo located in Pittsburgh, PA. The surroundings at this zoo are naturally appealing, which adds to the beauty of the photo. The zoo has always been one of my favorite places to visit. This particular visit was made by my entire family to celebrate a birthday. I remember watching this animal and being amazed by the calmness. "Lazy Afternoon" will leave an impression on my life forever.

RILES, LOUISE
I took this photograph from aboard the Circle Cruise Lines ship in New York on the way to Ellis Island and the Statue of Liberty. I was in awe of the beautiful profile of Manhattan. I didn't expect to get such a terrific shot. I'm just beginning to enjoy taking pictures of nature and beautiful scenery. I am looking forward to taking some photography classes.

RILEY, AMY
My name is Amy Chastity Riley. I am twenty-seven years old and from Sneedville, TN. This is a picture of my kitten, Tango, and his daddy, Issac. Tango had gotten up on my porch railing and could not get down. Issac just sat there looking at him as if to say, "Well, son, you got yourself up there; now let's see if you can figure out how to get down." I was fortunate enough to have had my camera in my hand. I am very proud of this picture. I want to share it with everyone.

RINGELING, J. LYNN
I love beluga whales. Their grace and beauty are breathtaking. As I watched this whale release his air bubbles, I thought it would make a great shot, but timing was everything. I had already tried several times to catch his bubbles, but to no avail. Just as I was about to leave the exhibit, I turned to take one more look and snapped this photo. In a flash, the moment was gone, but I knew I had captured something special.

RIVIEZZO, ROSE M.
This beautiful tulip had been in bloom for about a week, when in early April 2000, we got a surprise—overnight snowfall. I looked out my kitchen window in the morning and saw it stand-

ing so proudly, surrounded by snow, a kiss of it still lingering on its bloom. I grabbed my camera and ran outside to capture it on film. My husband, Fred, and I have three adult children—Alicia, Toni, and Geoff—and a precious six-year-old granddaughter, Gianna. They are the subjects of most of my photographs.

ROBERTS, BARBARA
This picture was taken on the Island of Dominica in the West Indies. Dominica is a volcanic island with rain forests covering the mountaintops. They have 365 rivers on the island, and this is one of them, called the Indian River. It was late afternoon when we were going down the river by rowboat, and I was photographing the reflections in the water. This shot turned out beautifully.

ROBINSON, LIBBIE
Our seven-year-old daughter, Meghan, was so excited to be able to use a real fishing pole! Her daddy was showing her the complicated use of the spin reel. He was having such a great time showing her how to use it that she quickly ran out of patience! This was our annual trip to Lake Tenkiller in northeastern Oklahoma. Tenkiller is famous for its excellent sand bass fishing, and every good fisherman knows that sunset is the best time to fish!

ROBINSON, MARSHA
When my stepdaughter, Emily, recently attended a benefit for the adoption of greyhounds, she bid on a lovely pink tutu provided by *Doggieduds.com* at the silent auction. When she came home and tried it on our dog, Rascal, not only did it fit, but Rascal seemed to enjoy wearing it! I was able to capture her with my camera in the outfit with a wistful expression that says, "Someday My Prince Will Come." We love catching Rascal with our camera in those memorable poses.

RODEN, VIRGINIA
My husband and I enjoy traveling and seeing the United States of America. We often head for Ennis, MT (where this photo was taken). The men in our family love trout fishing, and Montana is one of the best for fly-fishing. I love taking pictures and have gotten a reputation for taking crazy shots, so I often hear, "Watch out, here she comes." But I have a lot of fun and enjoyment. Some photos I threaten my grandchildren with, to show future spouses if they don't behave.

RODENBERGER, KAREN
This particular photo was taken on a ranch just north of LaGrange, WY, on a business trip to Stockman's Livestock in Torrington, WY. I took this photo because the windmills seemed to be a welcome call to the miles of ranch land. I have a lifelong passion for taking photos, not of anything in particular, although my children have been the main subject for years. Photos are my way of preserving the present and the past forever.

RODRIGUEZ, GLORIA L.
I have always liked taking pictures, since every moment captured in film is a memory frozen in time. For our fifth wedding anniversary we were on vacation by the sea. My husband, Adrian, and my daughter, Krystal, enjoyed watching the

seagulls. It was amazing to see them catch food in the air.

ROONEY, KATHLEEN McGAR

The roses were planted for my mother, Beverly, when she died. I was elated that they bloomed so wonderfully lush and profuse. So I took a picture and was surprised when it turned out so well. She would have loved the flowers and the picture! I used a new camera and was trying to get the hang of it. I have had more than a little success with it, so it was definitely money well spent.

ROOT, DARBY

This precious photograph is of my niece, Aeia. I have a strong passion for photography, and Aeia is a perfect subject. She fills our lives with so much joy that the moments I capture on film we can treasure forever. Along with family photography, my real love is landscape and scenery photography. I love taking pictures and capturing important moments in time that can be enjoyed for years to come!

ROSE, JULIE

I love to take pictures of anything—especially of animals, children, or anything in nature. If I have my camera with me, I will snap six or eight photos quickly, hoping one will come out perfect, instead of one picture that might blur or something. This picture I caught late one evening when the sun was going down. The trees cast just enough shadow to make it right. I love taking pictures.

ROSE, SUSAN J.

Nature, especially the animal kingdom, has a personality, emotion, and a sense of humor. Part of my enjoyment of nature photography comes from taking pictures of animal behavior that can be open to interpretation. Perhaps the viewer will find something to identify with or relate to, which will hopefully lead to a greater appreciation of the connection humans have to all of nature.

ROSENBERG, ADRIENNE T.

When I'm with my grandchildren, my camera is always loaded and hanging around my neck, ready for the spontaneity of the moment. The children's parents are usually too busy, with hands and attention otherwise occupied, to be able to savor the feeling of unfettered freedom. That's a grandparent's frequent reward and a wonderful way to be vigilant yet playful. While we were visiting an apple orchard, three-year-old Leo beckoned me to follow the resident geese, who obviously saw him coming. (The sign was an added surprise!)

ROSSI, SHEILA

Summers come and go quickly in Woodstock, IL. I had just finished a picnic with my two children, Steven and Michaelle Munger. The town park is not far from The Square. Soon this lovely pond would give way to snow and ice, where my children and so many others would be sledding and ice-skating.

RUBLE, MARCELLA J.

This photo shows one of the many nocturnal visitors to my wildlife cafeteria. Every night there are raccoons, foxes, and skunks. They love dog chow, peanut butter sandwiches, and hard-boiled eggs. They eat two hundred pounds of chow every three weeks in spring and summer when they bring their young. The daytime cafeteria feeds squirrels and hundreds of birds, from chickadees to quail. There are eight pans of fresh water for them. This half-acre in the redwoods is my sanctuary. It gives me great joy to share it with wildlife.

RUGGIERO, ROCKY

I love to photograph nature at its best. Its beauty is an act of God, meant to lift the hearts of those who gaze upon it. We find peace when viewing a setting sun in all its brilliance, a field of daisies untouched by human hands, a stand of white birch as a sun showers it with warmth and nourishment, or a waterfall so high that it seems to touch the sky as its clear crystal waters cascade upon the rocks below sending up a beautiful rainbow mist, dancing in the sunbeams that shine upon it. This is what I try to capture in my photographs.

RUHLMAN, BETTY M.

This is a photo of my grandson, Hunter Christian. Hunter is one of my sixteen grandchildren, and he's a real delight. I have used him as my model for many photos. I don't take photos that often; it is just a hobby.

RUSHING, JORDAN

I'm a sixteen-year-old student at Ridgeland High School. This was my first year with an interest in photography. I was on an outing with my church youth group. We were going to my Sunday school teacher's cabin on the lake. On the way up there, we came across these horses running through an open field. This picture shows the warmth and love that a mother has for her young and how safe we can feel around the ones we love.

SAGCAL, SANDY

This is a photo of the beautiful redwoods in Sequoia National Park, California. It was taken during a summer vacation to the area in the month of June. I am originally from Texas, and normally I don't see snow. Certainly, I did not expect to see snow in June. Everyone will see something different from pictures, but the reason I named this photo "Nature's Tranquility" is best summed up in the verse I gave it this past holiday season in Christmas cards I made and sent out: "May the holiday season help us reflect and bring us contentment, encouragement, and inspiration as we journey down new roads."

SAKOWSKY, HILDA

I've been around a photo lab since 1977 in Hbg. as a printer and packager, and I just decided to advance myself further with the help of my boss, just by his hints on how to take pictures. But the real understanding and knowledge came from God, whom I thank so dearly, and I thank you for selecting my first night shot for publication. I'm married, and I have two sons and one stepdaughter. They are proud of me.

SALCEDO, ANTONIO D.

In a moment of time, I took this picture from inside the cave. I was surprised that it came out so beautiful. I called it the "Radiant Wave" because it brings light inside the cave. This is God's creation. In our lives, when we are in the darkness, we will see the light of hope, love, and happiness.

SAMUELS, MANNIE

My wife and I are full-time RVers, traveling here and there. We are prolific photo buffs, taking pictures of everything. We do enjoy the water and found the Beaufort, SC, lighthouse a beautiful subject. We would love earning a small income taking these type of pictures.

SANDRITTER, BLONDALE

This is a print from a slide made in 1954 of our rec/living rooms. At that time, I was given my first 35mm camera, so I shot many rolls of film to learn how to set the camera (pre-automatic setting). I sought all sorts of objects to photograph for the effect of what I learned. As in everything worthwhile, goal direction pays off best. Oh, a lot of the slides hit the "circle file" before I gained self-confidence. The big portrait is of me at age twenty-one. The print is Renoir's *On The Terrace*.

SARRA, CHRISTOPHER

This is a picture of my niece, Nichole. Nichole was the greatest child for taking her picture. I took a lot of her. This one is special, the way she had the look of "nothing to it" while gushing the can. She is older now, but it's still a great picture. I have enjoyed taking pictures all my life, and everyone enjoys them. I tell them it is not me. It is a great camera.

SCARBOROUGH, TERESA

When my seventeen-year-old cat, Tessie, died, I was heartbroken. We adopted a new kitten who had been born the day after Tessie passed away. I wanted so much for our dog and the kitten to get along. Much to my delight, they love each other! I enjoy watching the two of them frolic and then snuggle together. I took this picture on a lazy Saturday afternoon while they both napped in the sun.

SCHEIDT, PAUL W.

This is a photo of my champion rooster, Flip, whom I raised since he was a day-old chick. He is a white-crested black Polish rooster from a breed of chicken mainly used for laying medium-large white eggs. We've shared many long conversations with each other (which I hope nobody ever heard), but I don't think we ever knew what the other one was ever talking about. I think when I was taking his picture, he was telling me to make sure that I got his best side. He's very particular, you know—but then again, so am I!

SCHENDEL, RICHARD

The little girl with the Popsicle is my granddaughter, Margaret Hazel Herman. She is two-and-one-half years old and is our seventh grandchild. The picture was posed by her aunt Lisa, who happened to be born on the Fourth of July at Fort Belvoir, VA, while I was in the service. The Fourth of July is a special day for our family, and we all try to get together on that date. Elaine and I have four children: Lisa, Dave, Lynne, and

Kristen, all married. I am known as Papa Dick, the family photographer.

SCHERRER, DANIEL
My wife, Kelly, and I were tired of paying the high prices for school pictures, and since I love taking photos of all things great and small, I decided to give this a shot. When we show off the photos of Bruce, age fourteen, and Richard, age thirteen, people ask what studio we use and are shocked to hear that I took them. I show off my boys every chance I get. We love them very much.

SCHICK, BETTY J.
Last September, my husband and I were on our way back from visiting with my dad and stepmom in St. Regis, MN. As we drove into Davenport, IA, we debated if we should stop there and eat or wait to eat when we got home. Home was another hour or so away. Well, we decided to stop and eat. After our meal we headed towards I-280. That was when we saw this beautiful sunset. I pulled over to the side of the road and took the picture. I am so glad we decided to stop and eat!

SCHICK, F. L.
This photo was taken with my inexpensive, small camera. Coming from Southern California, I visited my brother, Nick, and his wife, Theresa. They wanted me to see some beautiful areas near their home in North Carolina. I love to see majestic sights in nature, especially trees and waterfalls. Thank you for the opportunity of publishing my photo so others might enjoy it as I do.

SCHULTZ, MARJORY
It was a rainy, cold day in Upper Michigan. At about 4:00 P.M., the rain slowed down, and the sun came out. We had seen rainbows in the sky, and as the sun started to set, I was making our dinner and had just turned around to set the table. I saw the sun shining on the trees, and it looked like it was the pot of gold at the end of the rainbows that were there earlier.

SCHULTZ, RALPH T.
When taking a photograph, you don't really think about a large number of people seeing it. You see something that catches your eye, and then you aim and shoot. Maybe one or two people will see it; maybe no one will see it. The fall of 2000 was beautiful. I grabbed the camera and the wife, got into the car, and we were off on a Sunday drive. After stopping at the park and the zoo, I must have shot forty or fifty photos. After going through all the photos, "Peace" was the one photo that caught the eye of my daughter, Alanna, son, Josh, and my wife, Annette. I'm hoping this photograph will be enjoyed by all of you as much as we enjoy it.

SCHULZ, IRENE
Kona was dropped off in a box outside the door of the shelter. In freezing cold weather, they rushed her to the hospital, and she barely survived. When I adopted her, I was determined to gain her love and trust. Even though Kona enjoys her canopy bed, she still feels more secure sleeping with me. In her leisure moments she occupies herself with watching cartoons. Finally, after two years, I have succeeded in restoring her faith in mankind. She

used up one of her nine lives, and that's all she will ever use with me. This is just the beginning.

SCHWEIKART, RENEE
I have been an animal-lover since I was little. I cannot ever remember being without a pet. This is a photo of Tutie, the butterscotch, who is nine, and Noah, who is five. I also have a female cat named Alexus, who is nine, and a blue fronted amazon parrot named Peter, who is fourteen. They were all adopted, and I love them so much! They get along very well together, and they bring me a lot of companionship and joy. Their differences in personality are amazing to me, and, as you can see, Tutie occasionally has an attitude.

SCOTT, JODY
This is a photo of our sixteen-month-old granddaughter, Josie. She is taking time to smell the flowers in the garden as she helps Grandma Jody do the weeding. She loves the outdoors and always has a big smile for you. I'm so happy we got to share our special moment in the garden with everyone. We are so proud of our little smiley faces, and we'll cherish this picture forever. She is the daughter of Heather and Bob Rehmel of Mish., IN, of Lee and Jody Scott, South Bend, IN.

SEBESTA, JUNE C.
This collage of shopping pictures of Corpus Christi's Padre Staples Mall depicts a joyous time for young and old alike, since the holidays are always a special time, especially during the millennium celebration. I hope you like the picture and the memories.

SEVENICH, MARK P.
This photo captured different impressions for me. I had just returned home after voting on November 4. I sat on our front porch, enjoying the day. It was a gorgeous fall day filled with a warm Wisconsin breeze and vibrant colors that danced off of the sunlight. I found the bold colors of the American flag to be a striking contrast that meshed with the fluid colors of our maple tree and blue sky. To me, both images symbolized a time of transition. For nature, we were transitioning from fall into winter. For the country, we were transitioning from one president to another.

SHAH, AHMED IJAZ
My travels through North America took me to Yellowstone National Park, where I chanced upon a unique encounter with this magnificent animal that happened to wander onto the road. I have seen camels, cattle, and deer crossing rural roads in Pakistan, where I grew up, but never a bison. I'm sure my adventurous father, Javed, will enjoy this photo as would have my mother, Parveen, had she been alive. My elder brother, Shameryar, and younger brother, Shehzad, and his wife, Wajiha, can hopefully expect more photos like this one from my future travels.

SHEETZ, PAMELA
Zoe came to us almost three years ago on a rainy night. His mother had been killed by a truck, and our daughter, Eliza, brought him home. He was very tiny. He had to be fed with an eye dropper and taught to chew. As you can see, he has come a long way. He has brought great joy and happi-

ness into our lives. Knowing he has found such great comfort in his new family brings immense gratification that we have nurtured one of God's precious creatures.

SHEPHERD, MEGAN
The sky goes indefinitely in all directions, which alone speaks of the vastness and depth of God's love, not to mention the masterpieces God creates at sunrise and sunset. "The Heavens declare the glory of God; the skies proclaim the work of His hands" (Psalms 19:1). People ask, "How can you believe in God when you can't even see Him?" Let me ask this: have you ever seen the wind? I've seen the effects of the wind, but never the wind. If you want a visual sign of God, watch the sunset tonight. "Faith is the evidence of things unseen."

SHERMAN, CLIFFORD
I was trying to get some shots of the painter working on a blimp. The light was fading, and he was finished. On his way out, I stopped him and took this last shot on the roll. Whenever he does big jobs, he wears these shoes; they have gotten even more character with every job he does.

SHKILER, GITA
I immigrated to the USA seven years ago from the Ukraine. I spent one of my vacations in my home country. Among those people whom I wanted to see was my favorite college professor, Mrs. Dashkovsky. I was blessed to be one of her students. Her intelligence, civil courage, broad knowledge base, relentless pursuit of excellence from all her students, and parent-like attention to our lives made her a very special person in my life. She is ninety-one now, but she is still full of wisdom, energy, and plans. She is still a spiritual and moral beacon for me.

SHORT, BONNIE JO
I have had so much fun with this photograph. I took it about three years ago while heading east at sixty miles an hour towards Portland, OR, on Highway 26 coming home from the beach. A friend was driving, and when I noticed the gorgeous sunset, I rolled down the window and took the shot (I noticed the guard rail at the bottom). I was thrilled with such an extraordinary result from such a minimal effort. I have probably had about a hundred duplicates made over the years and am always so happy to offer it to friends, and they are always so grateful to receive it. Taking pictures is fun.

SHORT, DONALD
Matthew is our adopted baby. He just turned two years old. Casey was also adopted by us when Matthew was one year old. They are inseparable. My wife, Sandy, always has the camera loaded and is known as the family historian. We have taken thousands of pictures, all so unique that it was difficult to choose only one. This picture illustrates the epitome of their love and comradeship for each other. After this was taken, Casey joined Matt in the bathtub . . . without our permission! Our home is constantly a three-ring circus! We have four other grown children, all married, with children.

SILVANEY, EMMA JANE

The children pictured in my photo "Young Love—Precious Moment" are my great niece and nephew. They are Courtney and Kyle, twins, and they were two-and-a-half years old in this picture. I always enjoyed baby-sitting the young children in my family, and I always kept my camera handy. It's a great way to get spontaneous pictures. Young children are very unpredictable. I am a retired medical secretary, and I worked for a surgeon for many years. My favorite hobbies are amateur photography, painting country scenery, traveling, and gardening.

SINCLAIR, MEL

Thank you for providing the exposure for our photo; it's an honor. Our daughter, Cheryl, wanted to pick flowers for Mom. Thanks again for accepting us into the book *Vivid Exposures*.

SINNOTT, DARIA

During a memorable trip to Alaska to visit relatives, I was able to experience aspects of America's last frontier, which most tourists do not get to see. I stayed in a small town north of Anchorage. I remember many things about the trip. One of the most memorable was standing at a tiny airport in town and watching several small-engine planes, like the one in my photograph, take off into the skies as their pilots began their daily flight to work early in the morning.

SIRGIANNIS, BEVERLY J.

This is in memory of Suzie, who passed away two years ago at age sixteen. She was a blue torte Persian with lots of spark and a wonderful nature about her. Yes, animals do think, and they do have feelings. I always have my camera ready to take that special moment that my pets present.

SKAFAS, KERI

I love this photo. I took it while on an ambassador trip to Europe in 1999. I was twelve years old. We were told that this particular guard was in training. I tried my best along with some of my friends to get him to smile, and it worked. Although, as you can see in the background, he was being watched closely. I will always remember this trip and the friends I made along the way.

SKEENS, SANDY

One hot August morning, a party of seven headed for the sands of Myrtle Beach, SC. We were all excited to be getting away for a fun-filled vacation. Arriving in the late afternoon, we all headed for the beach. As we were soaking up the sun's rays, the sky began to cloud over. All of us found ourselves having to decide if we wanted to take a chance on getting wet, not wanting to leave the beach. I glanced to the right of me and stood in amazement as the clouds began to take form. The sun was shining in behind the clouds, and the light illuminated its glow. All of a sudden the dark clouds tried to cover the light. To my surprise they only helped to beautify this awesome scene. I came to my senses long enough to grab my camera and capture one of God's creations.

SKRIPOL, ROBERT A.

Abbie is our two-year-old black American shorthair. In the photo, she is inspecting the tulips that we purchased for Easter. The photo was taken in the morning sunlight shining through our kitchen window. We brought Abbie home as a very young kitten from a local animal shelter. We were told she was feral, found wandering the streets, and it took the animal control officer over a week to catch her. After a brief transition period getting used to each other, Abbie became the sweetheart of our household. She is a wonderful and precious young lady.

SLAY, CONNIE LYNN

While visiting my Canadian friends, I was voted to be on the bath team that night for their children, Andrey (six) and Matthew (seven). It was truly an experience not to be forgotten, as I soon realized the purpose of bathing was mainly to have fun and lastly to get clean. Little did I know that the bottle they told me to use was bubble bath. Needless to say, bubbles began to multiply and multiply, and the laughter of children rang throughout the house. With my camera ready for the unexpected, I captured Matthew sitting innocently in his end of the bathtub.

SLOYER, STANLEY D.

Travel and photography occupy a good part of my life. After retiring from thirty-four years in education, a summer job took me to Yellowstone National Park as a tour guide. I spend days off enjoying the natural wonders and incredible scenery both in Yellowstone and Grand Teton National Park, just a short drive to the south. My search for this early Mormon barn spanned seven summers. After failing to locate the elusive structure on my own, I finally admitted defeat and sheepishly asked a ranger for directions. So simple, but now aren't we supposed to ask for help?

SMITH, AMANDA LIN

I took this picture at a summer camp along Lake Bloomington, East Bay. I go to summer camps every year. During my sixth grade summer there, I took the picture "Inspiration Point" at sunset. My family and I thought it was beautiful. It is a great memory.

SMITH, BECKY

I am the retired great-grandmother of Mia Nicole. Though she is two years old, her passion is the love of books. Toys rarely amuse her. When I took her picture a year ago, I had no idea she would become a semi-finalist. I am not a shutterbug, but things like winter scenes of snow attract my attention. When I am not flipping shutters, my hobby is doing volunteer work.

SMITH, JAMES LEE

No, they are not the Smith brothers of cough drop fame. These brothers are, from left to right: my father, Jessie Lee Smith, Henry Smith, Marshall Smith, and Walter Smith. This photo was taken with an old box camera in about 1926, the year that I was born. Jessie, Henry, and Marshall all lived in west Texas, while Marshall resided in Farmington, NM. The Texas brothers were all farmers, and Walter was a blacksmith by trade. All are now deceased, with Jessie the last to go on June 4, 1971.

SMITH, LANIECE

When I took this photograph of clouds in the shape of an eagle, I asked my Native American friend if it had any meaning in their traditions. (Did you notice the face above the eagle's wing and the moon located in the forehead in the position of the "third eye"?) My friend said the photograph was to be named "The Messenger," and it's of the face of the guardian who sent the messenger. The messenger is telling us that the Earth is changing, that we are all feeling this, and that how we deal with it determines what happens.

SMITH, LAURIE JO

In this photo, my son, Brad, was so excited because it was just starting to snow for the first time that year. I wanted to capture the sheer joy on his face that day forever. One of my favorite hobbies is taking pictures of my family. Not only do my husband, Charlie, and I have a beautiful son named Brad, but we also have a beautiful baby girl named Emily Jo.

SOLLECITO, FRANK

I shot this photograph while vacationing in Arizona. Two friends and I were en route from Sedona, heading north to the Grand Canyon. The scenery was just absolutely incredible. This particular scene caught my eye primarily for the rich, golden blanket of sunlight, which had covered the entire foreground. There is a lot to be said for being in the right place at the right time and having your camera with you.

SPECTOR, LAURA

As an art teacher, I have always tried to teach my students to be observant and not to be afraid to try any art medium. I am a novice at photography but have always loved the work of Ansel Adams. His work was my personal inspiration. This photo is a memory piece. Twenty-two of us cruised to Alaska. It was a memorable trip in itself, but the beauty of Alaska is so magnificent that all I could do was hope I could capture its magnificence on film. I can't wait for my next trip and the photographs it will bring.

SPEICHER, CRYSTAL

After graduating high school in 2000, I went on a cross-country road trip with my brother and a friend. We took sleeping bags and a tent and stayed at the national and state park campgrounds from Pennsylvania to California. We saw some incredible sights along the way, but when we stayed at Mammoth Hot Springs in Yellowstone National Park, Wyoming, the views I saw were just breathtaking. It was sunset when I took this picture, and I remember saying to myself, "This is a moment I will never forget."

SPENCER, DONNA

This photo was taken on my birthday at Kartchner Caverns, just south of Phoenix, AZ. As a birthday gift, my girlfriend, Melissa, and I went out to enjoy the day. Little did we know, it would be a very cold and rainy day. This picture was taken just moments before the flood gates opened. It rained all day. My favorite hobbies are taking pictures of my family, going fishing with my husband, Curtis, and taking beautiful pictures of our Arizona sunsets.

SPOUTZ, PENNY
This was a vacation in the works for almost two years. We saw the Badlands, Mt. Rushmore, Devil's Tower, Yellowstone, and the Grand Teton Mountains. Twenty-two rolls of film later, I worried the whole trip if I really captured this beautiful shot. After a day of sight-seeing, we went back to Mt. Rushmore at night to see the presidents' heads lit up. People were running out of the park like a stampede because a storm was rolling in. So, my husband and I just went inside the first wall to take some photos of everything lit up; we didn't want to go any closer in case it really started to rain. The first few shots I took didn't turn out. I wasn't using a flash, and everything was washed out from the flood lights. But when the lightning hit, boy did it really light up the sky, and I did capture the shot of my life.

STANLEY, LISA M.
I have liked to take pictures since I was little. But one day, my mother and I were out, and I took my camera just in case I found something good to photograph. We came upon this beautiful waterfall. It just looked so peaceful. So I told Mom it looked like a good picture moment. I love taking pictures of nature and just being out in it because it brings about a very peaceful state of mind being in something so beautiful.

STEVENS, EUGENE C.
On a cold December morning, I climbed in the dark to a place called Vista Mound, which is north of Salt Lake City, UT. I waited until just the right moment to take this picture of a beautiful sunrise. Over the next hour I took several more pictures, which turned out just as nice. I love taking pictures of the outdoors, especially in the fall when the foliage is so gorgeous. I work at a convenience store, so I put my pictures on the counter for all of my customers to see.

STEVENS, JIM
This photographer has always been intent upon capturing the essence of the countryside on film, both in its ordinary, subtle beauty and in its extraordinary majesty. It is important to be aware of your surroundings as you travel, always being alert to sometimes fleeting opportunities. Man's stewardship of God's awesome creation by landscaping, building upon, and blending into it, is one of Jim's favorite themes. Jim has put hundreds of his photos on the web for enjoyment by all.

STOGSDILL, FRED
This picture was taken at Dale Hollow Lake and is named as is because even though it looks motionless, I am moving ten miles-per-hour in a canoe towards the viewer's left. In pictures, as well as life, there is more than one way to interpret a name. "Moving Stillness" could also apply to the water moving or to the picture moving the viewer.

STOVICEK, RICHARD
A little boy, his dog, and a sunny day in the park make the perfect ingredients for a heartwarming photo, which appeals to one and all. I was very happy to have had my trusty camera with me when I saw my young grandson, Noah Lausché,

sitting on the park bench looking lovingly at his protector and best pal, Einstein.

STROUD, NATALIE
I have hundreds of snapshots; however this one is so typical of my grandson. Baby-sitting has many advantages, with many opportunities to take adorable snapshots.

STROUP, ROCHELLE R.
From all my photographs of places I've been during the sixteen years I've served in the navy, this photo from my first sailing trip in Jacksonville, FL, is my favorite. It serves as a wonderful reminder of the great time we had watching the sunset upon leaving the landing. It added the perfect touch to the end of my trip by allowing me to share it with others.

STRUTHERS, JAMIE
As the sun slowly peeks its head over the plains and gently splashes its colors across the sky, I grab my camera, wipe the sleep from my eyes, and begin to shoot an amazing sunrise on the Serengeti Plains. Here they come, the migrating wildebeests, running in terror from the hungry alligators that rested just meters away at the waterhole. My heart races, as I know that I am capturing memories of a lifetime and incredible scenery that only a few lucky souls, like myself, are given the opportunity to experience.

STUCKEY, CONNIE R.
This was a beautiful Autumn day when I took my two children, Deane and Zachary, down to Jackson's Mill to enjoy the day and feed the fish in the pond. We do this often, but on this day it was beautiful and relaxing, the fall colors on the trees looking very pretty. I love the reflection off the water. It looks like a mirror. This is a famous area. It is connected with General Stonewall Jackson. We live about one mile from here.

STURGEON, LORRAINE
My grandmother loaned me her camera when I was twelve. I've enjoyed photography ever since. I especially like to take pictures of family and friends. My camera is never far from me. This is our great-granddaughter, Jacqueline. She didn't like the green apple. My husband and I have two sons, Rocky and Randy, two daughters-in-law, Chris and Lorna, and six grandchildren. Also there's our little Jackie.

SUAREZ ONATRA, FRANK JEFFREY
This is a photo of my dear uncle, Dr. William Onatra. I took this in the Santa Marta Beaches, Columbia, South America, at the beautiful sunset. "The Sun In A Hand" is the perfect name for that magnificent instant. I moved to Miami nine years ago with my mom, Betty, and my brother, Richard. I work in maintenance, and my hobbies are writing, reading, traveling, and taking nature pictures. I have a lot of them.

SWANN, JENNIFER L.
This is a picture of Kayla Shay McElyea, age four, daughter of Terry McElyea and Lanita Powers of Murfreesboro, TN. This picture was taken at the aquarium in Chattanooga, TN. It was summertime and very hot. The little ones

were playing in the fountains for relief, and I caught Kayla relieving her thirst as well. It was a good day for small pleasures.

TAMURA, JANET
I have been taking pictures for our church and putting them in the albums for over ten years. In Buddhist teaching, the spirits of the departed ones come back to Earth during Obon (traditional Buddhist memorial service) during the months of July and August. At the end of the season, thousands of toro, floating lanterns with the deceased's names written on them, are floated out to sea to return to Heaven. My husband and I have four grown children and four grandchildren. We live on the north shore of Oahu, Hawaii.

TAYLOR, LAUREL
Last August, I captured this photograph of a young moose while hiking with my friend, Walt Jordan, in the Wasatch Mountains around Snowbird, UT. I was delighted to get this close without using a telephoto lens. All morning, I had been looking for animals to photograph. Later, I found out that there is some risk because a moose can charge.

TEDFORD, NELL
I seem to have a green thumb and love flowers. I grew this flower in my front yard. I admired the beauty, and I thought it needed to be photographed. I am an eighty-four-year-old mother of two daughters, grandmother of six, and great-grandmother of eight. I am not really into taking many pictures, but I'm realizing it is a very interesting hobby.

THOMAS, KYLE B.
This photo was taken with a Nikon N905 last July in London. I was struck by the beauty of this asymmetrical statue while sight-seeing. It was complimented by the brilliant and celestial effects of the sun and the clouds. Because it was the last exposure on my roll, catching it on film was especially rewarding for me.

THOMAS, MARIE T.
The title of my photograph comes from what I think tortoises believe—that it's better on the other side! They are very determined and will not give up no matter what they are trying to conquer. My camera is always loaded and close by, so I can capture these moments. My boyfriend, Ronnie, and I share a home with fourteen desert tortoises. Ten are babies, and four range from ages three to five years. They are wonderful creatures and fun to watch grow.

THOMPSON, TRACY
Look at that face! This is Peaches. Isn't she precious? My husband, Erick, and I have had the joy of having Peaches for approximately one year. There isn't a day in our lives that she doesn't brighten our day. This photo is one of my favorites because it portrays her as I normally see her. She loves to sit at our front door and look outside. This is her favorite pastime, other than sleeping! We hope this photo puts a smile on your face, as she does ours every day!

TIRONE, LAUREN M.
I have always had an interest in picture-taking, even as a small child. I suppose I got it from my grandfather, who loved to set up the slide projector when family visited. This photo is of my cat, Kylie, whom I adopted from the local SPCA. Kylie is a true ham and loves to pose for her picture.

TITUS, SANDY
Ever since I was a little girl, I have always had a camera in my hand. I look for unusual settings and try to capture unique moments in time. Indescribable scenes slip away all too quickly, only to be recorded through the eyes of the beholder. This is an exceptionally breathtaking view of Cumberland Falls, KY.

TODD, KIMBERLY
When I look at something as magnificent as this sunset, I believe it's God speaking directly to us. If we choose to listen over the noise in life, we go beyond the routine and the ordinary. When we can touch that part of ourselves that reveres something bigger than our own feelings and needs, we connect to a reality that makes even a sunset a blessing. I believe we are all children of God! He wants only the best for us, in this life and the next!

TOEWS, GEORGETTE M.
This scene presented itself while I was on a windjammer sailing trip off the coast of Maine. As soon as I observed the natural (unposed) arrangement of articles on this beach, I felt I had to capture the moment. It represents the calm, serenity, and simplicity of life on the coast. The trip was a retirement gift to myself after thirty years in the United States Air Force, and it fulfilled every expectation I had about this beautiful part of the country.

TOLBERT, JOHN
The photo shows our son, John, in action on his four-wheeler. He is riding near our home, where there is a creek he crosses while blazing the trails. John and his twin sister, Emily, both love the thrills and excitement of riding. They are very safe and careful riders, but they love catching some air when they top a hill, as well as making some spray when they cross the creek. We are very proud of John's riding abilities, and we're really excited about seeing John's picture published. Keep on riding and have a great time. We love you!

TRIPPE, DONNA JOAN
The spring of the year 2000 was our very first for the wood duck house, and, of course, I wanted some pictures. But I wasn't very sure how lucky I would be. I had almost given up hope for a tenant when Mrs. Woodduck arrived. I would go down to our dock and softly talk to her before trying to open the lid to look inside. She was with us for about twenty-nine days and produced sixteen eggs and allowed me to take several photos of her with her family. Within twenty-four hours of the first egg hatching, she and her ducklings were gone from the nest, never to be seen again.

TROMBINO, IRENE
In June 2000, we took the Perillo Tour of Israel. The Caves of the Dead Sea Scrolls were among the many picturesque and historical sights seen and of which many pictures were taken. I thought this one was the most beautiful.

TROTT, SHELLEY
I live in an area where wildlife is abundant, although this picture was taken while we were on vacation! I've always loved to take photographs of family, friends, and especially wildlife. This pair amazed me because they didn't look real! There was no movement other than the throats when they breathed. I really enjoy pictures that are both ordinary and unusual. I love to try to capture the feeling of being there. I also wish to pass on to my two children and others the art of expression through pictures. I so enjoy that myself.

TROUT, KATHLEEN V.
My husband, Richard, and I spent our first five years in an old house facing this barn. We then moved down to the farm where his father had farmed. Now we are back near this barn in a new house. With the old tractor in front of the barn and the falling leaves, I thought it might make a good picture. Our oldest son, Tony, farms the farm with the help of our other two sons, Tim and Todd. Our daughter, Debbie, lives at the end of our farm lane. We have six grandchildren and two great-grandchildren.

TROY, SUZANNE
This is a photograph of Phipps Conservatory in the Oakland section of Pittsburgh. The building is a wonderful greenhouse, built in the 1800s. It has many rooms that are decorated with exotic plants and many varieties of flowers. It is my sanctuary. I am only able to visit Phipps once a year in the warm summer months. I have a very painful type of nerve damage that has paralyzed my right side and permanently disabled me. It's called reflex sympathetic dystrophy (RSD). This condition has left me very weak, and functioning is very difficult. There is no cure for RSD. When I go to Phipps, I take many pictures. I have them framed throughout my home. They give the encouragement of spring and remind me every day that there is always beauty in life if you know where to look.

USARAGA, NECIAS E.
Photography is my hobby. Whenever possible, I always take my camera with me. This photo is of the Philippine tourist spot called Chocolate Hills. Several similar hills are all around. On top of the tallest hill is a lovely restaurant that overlooks the whole area. Tourists and visitors frequent here just to see the beautiful scenery and to have some souvenir pictures. I took one too. My husband, Rene, and I are both registered optometrists, Philippine graduates. We have one daughter, Cherry Faye. We own an optical clinic in the Philippines.

VANCE, TERESA
I usually keep my camera close by, especially at family gatherings. I had just finished cutting the watermelon and was taking the knife into the kitchen when my dad called for me to get my camera. I picked it up off the bar, walked out, and snapped a couple of pictures. My eleven-month-old daughter, Taylor, who had just recently learned to walk had been watching everything with great interest. And since I didn't give her a piece of watermelon, she decided to walk over and get it herself.

VILENDRER, GERALD J.
We raised a flock of mallards one summer when we lived in Minnesota. We got the ducks when it was too cold to keep them outside, so they initially stayed inside in a child's wading pool in our basement. Our German shepherd, Hansel, was curious and used to circle their pool, and the ducklings became accustomed to him. When the ducks moved outside, Hansel would herd the ducklings in the yard, and they easily accepted his protection. Hansel was never aggressive toward the ducks, which were eventually given their freedom at a lake in a nearby park.

VOGT, CHRISTINE M.
On a beautiful, sunny day in April, my boyfriend and I were visiting the Philadelphia Zoo. While in the lorikeet enclosure, I looked up and saw these two lovely birds sitting on a branch. I was quite pleased at how well this picture turned out using my automatic camera. I'm an x-ray technologist by trade, but I seem to have a knack for taking nice photographs. Who knows? Maybe I'll become a professional photographer one day. I love taking pictures.

WADE-GOODE, MARTISTINE
This is a picture of two-and-a-half-year-old Ariel Layla putting lotion on herself after putting it all over her exhausted grandma. Her lotion is actually baby powder, and the camera was ready in the nick of time to catch her in the act.

WAGNER, TODD
I am drawn to the ocean for its beauty, danger, mystery, and romance. Nothing is more exhilarating than being on the beach at night with the wind blowing and the moon shining on the water. I love to think of what is happening under the surface of that vast ocean. When I walked out of the cottage and saw Mom sitting there, I knew it would make a special picture. This "Peaceful Moment" is filled with thoughts of peace, serenity, and wonder.

WAKEFIELD, CAROL
Dale Quaife, my son, was barbecuing steaks on his deck. It started raining. He grabbed an umbrella to keep the steaks dry. I snapped this picture through the patio door. Our whole family loves to take pictures. My husband and I spent our holiday with Dale and his family in Oshawa, Ontario, Canada, where this picture was taken. This is the first time I have entered my picture in a contest.

WALDRIP, SUZIE
This is a photo of Rusty as he first ventured outdoors. I saved Rusty from the Roswell Humane Society. He was sickly as a kitten but soon grew to be strong and healthy. I get my love for photography from my father, who always had a camera in his hand while I was growing up. I am a second grade teacher, and I enjoy taking pictures of people when they're not posing. I like to show my young students how to use a camera and see the beauty of life through the eyes of one another.

WALLICK, LISA
We traveled to Alaska to participate in the Major's Midnight Sun Marathon. We were running for Andrew. We hoped in some way we would honor his courageous battle against leukemia and encourage public awareness. In your loving memory, Andrew, this picture will always be a reminder of your innocent beauty and majestic spirit.

WALTON, CLARENCE
I caught this shot after visiting the new historical museum and park in Orlando, FL. The timing was perfect with the bus in the background and the liz-art statue. What it said to me was, "I am the head of this odyssey (trip)." Images of a fantasy filled my head.

WARNER, LINDA E.
I took this photo of my son, Curtis (center), and two of his closest friends when we went to an amusement park for his sixth birthday. When we got on a train ride I asked them to turn around. The look of excitement on their beautiful faces was priceless. These three kids were inseparable all summer. About a year later, the two girls moved away. Curtis is now nine years old, and every time he sees this photo he says he really misses them. This is a great way to keep a little piece of his childhood memories around forever.

WAY, ALLAN R.
This photograph of my daughter was taken for her pre-wedding collection, as she tried on her gown for the final fitting. Her dog, Otis, uncoaxed, walked over to her and sat down on her dress with a rather inquisitive look on his face. I am a freelance photographer specializing in commercial photography.

WEILERT, LOIS
I am a mother of four and a grandmother of five with another one on the way. This is a photo of my son, Brett, showing my grandson, Tommy, a good time. When they are together, I can always get an action photo. I am delighted that you enjoy my photography.

WEIMMER, LINDA
This picture was taken on our honeymoon. My husband, Richard, whom everyone calls Papa, and my granddaughter, Emma, whom we call Eber, were riding a camel for the first time. We were at the Texas Renaissance Festival, which we love. We dedicate this picture to my mother, Juanita, who died the same year this picture was taken. The picture taken is of me, Linda, and my daughter, Becky, who also accompanied us on our honeymoon. It was a great time.

WELSH, ANNE
This photo was taken on a tranquil country road between Fort William and Oban, Scotland. People often initially think it is a painting because of the muted reflection of the sky and clouds in the water. The moment was obviously perfect in terms of the isolated setting, the lighting, and the time of day. I was incredibly lucky to arrive at just the right time . . . with my camera in hand!

WELSH, BETTY M.
I stopped at a pumpkin farm, and while there I noticed a huge pumpkin by a shed. Instantly, I went to the car for my camera. When I was ready to take my photo, a cat appeared in the scene as if to say, "Take my picture too." It was an awesome and thrilling experience, one of the joys I receive with photography as my hobby.

WESTON, JOELYN
I love to step outside after a spring rain. When I went outside this time, it was dusk, and this beautiful cloud was there to greet me. After getting the pictures developed, I noticed the faces in the clouds.

WHEELER, SANDRA KAY
God has blessed my husband, Todd, and I with six beautiful children—three boys and three girls. Having all of them within six years, they are all close, and each girl was blessed with an older brother. This picture captures the very essence of my daughters. Since they are all home-schooled, I am fortunate to be surrounded with these angels twenty-four hours a day. I am truly blessed!

WHITMER, MARY L.
This photo of Woogie was taken Thanksgiving Day 2000. Woogie and his brother, Boogie, were seven months old and had never eaten people food. After being pestered all day by them smelling the turkey cooking, I gave in and gave them some. I believe the picture captures just how much they enjoyed it.

WHITTLE, SARAH C.
Buck Wheat, our yellow Lab, always enjoys our trips to Abaco, Bahamas, to relax in our home and enjoy the ocean. He has many frequent flier miles and is a great, well-behaved eleven-year-old. He goes to work with me every day, and my customers drop in just to visit with Buck Wheat. He even made the local paper. He's a great dog friend. I am an RN, a salvage coworker, and an amateur photographer.

WIGDERSON, WYNNE
Spending my summers at Paw Paw Lake in Michigan, my whole life it has been impossible to describe the beauty of the lake to anyone. This picture does it without words. This has special meaning to me. My grandparents started vacationing at the lake in 1908 and bought a cottage there in 1935. My mother now owns a home on Paw Paw Lake, where I took this photograph. My husband, Jim, and I live in Pensacola, FL, and visit my mother, Edythe, at the lake as often as possible.

WILBURN, RICKY
This is a red-tailed hawk; it likes the water plant here where I work in Cleveland, OH. It hunts for rabbits here and all kinds of rodents. There are also crows here that compete for its prey. They will attack the hawk, but it will stay until it finds its prey. Seeing one in the air is like seeing perfection at work. It makes coming to work a real joy. To be around so many man-made buildings and to see nature at work is like getting two paychecks, only one pays more.

WILLIAMS, GAY J.
"Peek-A-Boo" is a picture of my second dalmat-ian, Perdy Girl. She came to me shortly after the death of my first dal, Ladybug. Perdy's first three years were spent being passed from owner to owner before finally ending up in the local pound, where I adopted her. She was very shy and unsure of me, and I was leery of taking on a new pet so soon. As she becomes more secure in her new permanent home her sweet personality is emerging. We are healing each other. This is my first non-concert photo to be published.

WILLIAMS, JASMINE
I love taking pictures! I see the beauty and specialness in the magical moment of a photo I'm about to take. I love to capture that moment. I saw the look of love and happiness on my son's face; he was so content and alright with the world on that summer day. The sun was warm and inviting, and he had just learned to walk a few days earlier. His sister, Maria, is very protective of her little brother, and rightly so. He is such a sweet little boy. His name is Xzavier. He also has an older brother, Rafael. I work at home in giftware and photography; sometime after this, though, I may be taking more pictures!

WILLIAMS, MERLE
I am currently a student of photography at the Massachusetts College of Art. My work is varied, but consists primarily of human figure studies. This photograph was inspired by that focus. I wanted to convey a personification of the flower by displaying its basic figure.

WILLIAMS, TRACY W.
When I saw this photograph for the first time, my heart pounded! Racing up Split Rock at Grandfather Mountain in Linville, NC, I was able to capture not only the beautiful rays of the sun shining through the clouds, but also a beautiful silhouette of my children with an awesome starburst effect. It reminds me that in the everyday struggles of life, if we will just search for the light, we will find it. No matter how unfixable things may seem, there will always be a spark that remains that can rekindle new life in us. Thus the title, "Ray Of Hope."

WILLIAMS, ZAKIA
I took this picture while riding in the back seat of our rental car on our trip to Atlanta. I am still surprised at the way this picture turned out. I took a photography class in high school, and I think that the class really helped me understand what photography is about. Even though photography isn't my major in school, I do enjoy it as a hobby. I am eighteen years old and will be a freshman in college in the fall of 2000.

WILLIS, SARA
This is a photo of Everette Dunagan's grocery and supply store in Monticello, KY. Lake Cumberland brings many tourists to this area every year. Many visit the store because of its rustic appearance. This quaint little country store has served the public since the 1930s. I am a junior at the University of Louisville. In the fall of 2000 I had a chance to take photography. Since I'm a nursing major, I considered it my stress release class. Since then I have developed a great respect

for photography and the photographers who take the time to make their work beautiful.

WINDSOR, RICHARD F.
Every Fourth of July at 10:00 P.M. the land owners around the perimeter of Chautauqua Lake light flares placed at fifteen-foot intervals. Then the various communities set off fireworks to produce a uniquely patriotic American experience.

WOLCOTT, JEANE M.
It would be difficult to describe Sneakers in a hundred words or less. He belonged to my parents, and I inherited him on their passing. Sneakers was my first cat, so we had many words about his behavior and mine. We finally had a meeting of the minds. . . . I yelled; he talked back. It was a satisfying arrangement. Suffice to say, he was a wise-guy, smart beyond belief and very affectionate. At eighteen years of age, he had the last word. Gone but never forgotten.

WOLF, YAEL
[b.] May 31, 1985; [p.] Dennis and Elise Wolf; [ed.] 7th grade, Castillero Middle School; [occ.] Middle School Student; [hon.] President's Award 1996, honors student; [pers.] I love animals; I always have. I like taking photos. I think it is cool looking back on special moments in my life.

WOLSEGGER, HOPE ROBSON
How wonderful it would be if we could all take time to allow for "Falling Down In Leaves." I waited many years to have children and was absolutely astounded at how this little beauty changed me, how I see everything in our world like it is the first time again. These feelings inspired a photography session of her "Falling Down In Leaves." I have had a twenty-year passion for photography. Makaela boosted this passion and gave me a willing subject—herself. Photographs are glimpses into our most precious moments.

WOODALL, MELISSA
I love taking walks on lovely days or camping under the sky. This photo was taken at local mountains in Virginia when I was hiking in the fall. It is entitled "Diamond In The Rough" because amidst all the dead trees this one was bright and colorful—very much alive!

WRIGHT, MARY ANN
Positive, accountable, and caring, TTI, Inc. is a company standing on the far northeast side of Fort Worth, TX. A portion of the building was added on in the year 1995. TTI, Inc. is mounted and stands firm on a solid rock foundation. A face with a frown and the spirit of Jesus Christ dwell in the midst. May the owner, Paul Andrews, and family be blessed in every way. Corporate managers and supervisors, co-workers, and associates, such as Min. R.L. Wright, Tialonda, Tyalicia, Tamiko, Twila, Rotarian, Shaunee, Corey, and Michael are all blessed as well. I pray that prosperity flows throughout TTI, Inc., worldwide in Jesus' name.

WYATT, TAMI
My boyfriend, Dan, and I were visiting Washington, DC, from Florida. On an exceptionally cold and snowy day, we trekked out to see the National Monument and reflection pool. As we walked, holding hands, the still silence grew heavier, and you could hear each snowflake hit the ground. I looked ahead and saw a single set of footprints coming toward us and felt as if we were being greeted by something spiritual. The splendor of the enveloping blanket of snow was the most beautiful sight and was very romantic.

YATES, MARY LOUISE
My abyssinian cat, Chesapeake (Chessie for short), loves to eat, and he will do most anything to get my attention—even sitting in the pantry closet. As a retired nurse I have much time on my hands, during which I can take photographs. Our five cats—two abysinnians, one Havana brown, and two Heinz Fifty-seven varieties—are always into something, and this time I was able to capture this picture before Chessie moved on to bigger and better things.

YOUGH, MATTHEW
Hi, I'm Jamie Wilson. This picture was taken by my friend, Matthew Yough of Saxonburg, PA, on our cross-country trip in September 2000. Washington State was so unlike anything we'd ever seen, and Matt suddenly had me pull over on U.S. 90 to "get a shot of that house." My mother, Jeri Wilson, loved it and sent it to you, and here we are! It's a special memory. We all had a part in composing this book.

YOUNG, WILLIE J.
The Peacock Bridge is located near a city in Alabama call Alexander City. I grew up not far from it. My brothers and I played near it and fished there too. The bridge was built in 1931, before I was born. It became very interesting to me in later years—how it was built and the rocks in the bed of the river. So I decided to photograph it from a different angle.

ZAHER, J. E.
This is a photo of my two granddaughters, Madison and Taylor, taken at Ripley's Sea Aquarium, viewing the jellyfish in amazement. They were hypnotized by the way the jellyfish moved through the water. I used 400 speed film and a Minolta X-700 set on auto with flash fill-in. I enjoy taking portrait photos and action shots of my grandson, Adam, playing baseball or golf. My favorite lens is the 70-210 tele-zoom. For portrait shots the subjects never realize their picture is being taken.

ZAUN, SANDRA
This picture was taken while traveling through the small town of Iron Gate in the midwestern part of Virginia. The river seen is the James River. The photo was taken in October when the leaves were at their peak. I enjoy taking pictures of nature's wonders and anything else, especially people. I am always the one behind the camera. I have photos of every trip, every person, and every event in my life. Someday, I hope to become a professional photographer.

ZIMMERMAN, PATSY C.
My husband and I travel quite a lot, and I take a lot of photographs. But it is really exciting when a scene presents itself as though it's waiting just for my camera. In this instance, we, with three friends and a guide, were touring Pompeii when we walked past the end of the one-block-long street. Our timing was perfect for the sunshine and shadow composition.

INDEX OF PHOTOGRAPHERS